Conscience

To Michael
with best wishes
from

[signature]

Conscience

Ethical Intelligence for Global Well-Being

MARTIN PROZESKY

UNIVERSITY OF KWAZULU-NATAL PRESS

Published in 2007 by University of KwaZulu-Natal Press
Private Bag X01
Scottsville 3209
South Africa
E-mail: books@ukzn.ac.za
Website: www.ukznpress.co.za

ISBN-13: 978-1-86914-097-7

Managing editor: Sally Hines
Editor: Alison Lockhart
Typesetting: Patricia Comrie
Cover photograph: David Prozesky
Cover design: Flying Ant Designs

Printed and bound by Interpak Books, Pietermaritzburg

Contents

Preface

Globalisation sets alarm bells ringing for many people because they experience it as a threat that is taking several forms. These include the ability of the United States of America to impose its military power on most of the world at will, ruthless transnational corporations driving the little guys out of business, and the rising danger of serious global warming.

How can anxious, caring people meet such massive challenges? How can the 'Davids' of conscience overcome the 'Goliaths' of greed and violence, when all they have is the set of regionally confined moralities – those of our various, separate faiths and philosophies – that mark the present world situation? How can we meet wide-reaching evils with the merely provincial and patriotic systems of ethics that history has given us? How can we overcome a united foe with a fractured human conscience?

The answer is that we cannot. Only a genuinely shared global conscience, which practises a set of core values, can meet the worldwide dangers besetting us. Since a global conscience does not yet exist, the greatest ethical challenge of our times is to create it. This book offers a contribution to that process, a process already underway in a few parts of the world, as will be seen in Chapter Four. It does so by focusing on the massive potential of an informed, inspired and active conscience to become a global force for good, such as the world has never seen before.

Thus the book calls for a global ethical revolution that religious and secular people can all bring about as equals. To this great project, *Conscience* offers resources of heart, head and hands, drawing freely on the vast heritages of moral wisdom and experience around the world, as well as on personal experience in one of the most ethically charged contexts of recent times – South Africa, in the transition from apartheid to democracy.

While the book rests on extensive scholarly work extending over the past 25 years and more, it is written for the thoughtful general reader and not for academic specialists. And while it draws on and explains the ideas of many of the world's greatest ethics teachers, the main emphasis is practical, showing how in practice, good people can become even better, and how whatever is not yet good, can be changed for the best.

Hilton
South Africa
February 2006

Acknowledgements

When a book draws on many years of experience, study and interaction, its debt to others will naturally surpass conscious memory of them all, and hence also the ability to thank them by name. What I can do is acknowledge those who in various ways helped me during the process of writing and revision: by reading the work in progress, in part or whole, and giving me comments, suggested improvements and encouragement; by taking part in the many ethics workshops I have facilitated, and by attending and responding to my lectures over the years. Most of the latter have taken place at the former University of Natal in South Africa, and more recently at its successor, the University of KwaZulu-Natal, as well as at various other centres in Britain, the United States of America, Australia and New Zealand.

I mention these mentors, friends and colleagues now in alphabetical order with deep gratitude: Michael and Jonathan Bands, John Baxter, John B. Cobb Jr., Rex Finch, Lloyd Geering, Pumla Gobodo-Madikizela, Brenda Gourley, Kate and Jack Kallis, Larry Kaufmann, Ron Nicolson, Jonathan Reiber, Hays and Linda Rockwell, Stewart Sutherland, Trevor Williams, and Jacquie Withers.

I would also like to extend my thanks to the readers of my local newspaper, *The Witness*, who so helpfully responded to my request for views about the qualities of a good person in September 2004. That I disagreed with a few of the many suggestions I received, in no way diminishes my appreciation.

A special word of thanks goes to Desmond Tutu. With typical generosity of spirit, the emeritus Archbishop agreed to read the manuscript at what was an extremely busy time for him. The kind words he wrote for the back cover of this book mean more to me than I can say.

Thanks are also due to the University of KwaZulu-Natal and its predecessor for supporting my work in comparative and applied ethics, and to the governing bodies of Trinity College, Oxford and The Open University for enabling me to spend a sabbatical in Britain, researching parts of this book.

I am also very grateful to the Unilever Foundation for Education and Development and The Atlantic Philanthropies for their generous financial and moral support for the Unilever Ethics Centre at my university and its African Ethics Initiative, which it has been my privilege to launch and direct since 1998. Ed Hall and Michael Savage have been especially supportive throughout. My colleagues at the Unilever Ethics Centre have been a genuine dream team of deeply committed applied ethicists, to whom I will always be very grateful.

To Glenn Cowley and Sally Hines of the University of KwaZulu-Natal Press, and to the editor, Alison Lockhart, I also owe a debt of thanks for their highly professional handling of this book.

And as always, my wife Elizabeth, and our sons, Justin and David, have been wonderfully supportive of my efforts, enriching them in ways too many to mention. In a very real sense, they are the heart and soul of the present work.

This Book in Brief

- This book calls for a renaissance of conscience, a new ethical genesis in a globalising world of superb potential for greater flourishing, brought about by democracy and the information age, but also beset by grave, and at times, worsening problems. The most serious are greed, poverty, the new imperialisms of the United States of America and giant corporations, fundamentalisms, religious bigotries, gender injustice, damage to the environment and the inadequacies of our inherited value-systems.
- Our traditional value-systems rest too much on moral passivity and obedience, and on elitist and male-dominated interpretations of the good. Some of them are harmed further by a Western bias and by incomplete accounts of basic ethical values.
- Conscience must now become a global force for good, or we could well be gravely damaging ourselves and the natural environment that is our only lifeboat, and without which we have no future.
- To become such a force, conscience, which I also speak of as 'ethical living' or 'morality', must find a new and genuinely inclusive basis and motivation. We can find these in the human nature we all share and in our common membership of an interrelated world.
- Ethical living at every level – from the individual to the global – is the only way to achieve what we all want most: the deepest, richest and most sustainable well-being.
- This view is based on the realities of our human nature, our human experiences of deep moral value, and on the reality of an inter-connected world and universe, backed up by science, philosophy and religion at its best.

- In working for a new age of conscience, we must proceed ethically, for ethics is as much about appropriate process as it is about sound values. Above all, this means that we must proceed on the basis of maximum inclusiveness, welcoming creative moral insight and effort from everyone.
- The creation of a better world of the future must be the work of all of us together as moral equals. There are no moral superpowers, but there can be moral super-citizens. A truly global ethic demands nothing less of us all.
- While this book is passionate about maximum inclusiveness and the ideal of a truly global conscience, no single writer can validly claim to see the moral world in the way that astronauts see Earth from space – complete and whole. Nonetheless, the 'South-Western' perspective from which it comes – meaning a perspective that formed in southern Africa, but is also rooted in the developed world, in Britain, Australia, New Zealand and the United States of America – is enriched and extended by the moral wisdom and values of the East as well.
- At the heart of human goodness, of a life fired by conscience, are generosity, harmlessness and truthfulness as the right and good way to manage our daily lives at all levels – personal, familial, organisational, national and global. Human nature, science and our variegated moral heritage all support this contention, which logically leads to a set of core values that provide specific details for the content of ethical living.
- The ethics explored in this book must be realistically in touch with the most influential realities of twenty-first-century existence (some of them are assets; others are serious liabilities) if we are to make conscience the heart and soul of the future.
- Given the challenges of our times, the creation of a new ethic for a new global era calls for the spirit and style of the pioneer, not the settler. It calls for ethics in creative mode, not obedience mode, involving a fresh and inclusive approach to some timeless values.
- This is a project for every citizen and every leader. Its central skill is humane, truthful management of ourselves and our institutions, based on understanding, motivation, commitment and action, celebrating

and furthering the good in life, transforming the evil, and knowing how to handle what is perhaps life's most important question: how will we relate to others?

- It is a project for realistic achievement, not a call to sainthood; it seeks a better world, not a utopian paradise.
- These contentions involve four great questions:
  1. What can provide humanity with a firm foundation for a global conscience?
  2. Why do greed and selfishness fail?
  3. What values does ethical living involve?
  4. How can we enhance the power of conscience?
- Chapter One sets the scene, and Chapters Two to Five offer some ways of thinking about answers to these four questions.

one

Well-Being, Conscience and a World in Trouble

HOPE FOR THE FUTURE

Conscience is the only passport to what we all want most: the richest and most durable well-being. It is a self- and potentially world-transforming power that chooses generosity over greed, truthfulness over lies, and love over indifference. Its home is the innermost, deepest part of us, which I think of as the soul. From there, it radiates outward to transform our communities, organisations, cultures, nations and planet – if we can only energise it and set it free. Conscience brings together wisdom, values and truths, without which, nothing can truly flourish and endure, and unites what our separate cultures divide. It is not afraid of sacrifice and thrives on tough challenges. Conscience – and conscience alone – can be the foundation of a lasting future of global flourishing, but only if we make it richer, deeper and stronger than ever before.

This, in a few sentences, is the message of this book. It invites readers to help in building the foundation for greater global flourishing, setting out all that its author has learnt about the potential of our sense of right and wrong, good and evil, to dethrone the greed, violence, narrowness and lies that plague our existence.

Does this sound like a mere pipedream? Yes, it might – until we remember the reality of a Gandhi or a Nelson Mandela and the countless

1

others who have proved to us that great generosity of spirit and action are a reality, not an illusion.

For me, the experience of a conscience embracing all creeds and cultures began during my boyhood. We were very active Christians and when I was eight, we moved to a town with a large Jewish community. As I grew up, I developed a deep, lasting friendship with a Jewish classmate, and friendly links with others of my age from the same community. This gave me a window into the beliefs and values of Judaism, which my parents encouraged. I met people of great integrity and warmth, driven by a faith that traditional Christians see as mistaken and as surpassed by theirs. Later, at university, I met Buddhists, atheists, Muslims and Hindus for the first time, and was often struck by their fine qualities of honesty and kindness. These experiences took me further and further from the world of exclusive doctrine and towards an inclusive conscience.

ENLIGHTENMENT FROM A ROAD ACCIDENT

The importance and beauty of a moral sense embracing all creeds and cultures became painfully but unforgettably clear some years later, one winter morning during the heyday of apartheid in South Africa, the country of my birth. In those days, as a young academic without much money, I travelled to work on a much-loved motor scooter. I was on my way to the university campus, enjoying the lively zip of the bike as I throttled up a road past a row of modest suburban houses in what was then a whites-only neighbourhood. Suddenly a small fox terrier appeared from a nearby gate and rushed out at me, barking wildly.

Instantly I knew that I had to brake and swerve, or hit and probably kill the animal. Instinct took over and I braked – but too strongly. The bike lurched sideways, enough to miss the dog, but also enough for the bike to go down, sending me flying. As I fell, one of the rubber handlebar grips struck me above the left eye, just under my crash helmet. The skin burst open and blood poured down my face.

Badly shaken, but with no broken bones, I stood up slowly. The dog was nowhere to be seen, doubtless satisfied by the score of Dogs: 1, Humans: 0. With blood running down my face and the fallen bike at my feet, I must have looked a mess. I also needed help immediately for my gashed eyebrow. The incident took place long before cell phones, so I was dependent on passers-by.

Nobody emerged from the nearby houses. A few cars passed me, driven by whites like me. Then another car pulled up nearby. A dark-skinned man and woman got out and hurried towards me, members of my province's large community of people with forebears from the Indian sub-continent. I vividly remember the red dot on the woman's forehead, a custom of the Hindu community to signify marriage. The man gave me a neatly folded handkerchief to press to the cut over my eye, and to wipe the blood from my face, pulled my bike to the sidewalk, and shepherded me to the car.

It was then that I noticed that it was a taxi. Under apartheid laws at that time, it was a taxi for 'non-whites', and carrying me was against the law. But without hesitation, my two Indian benefactors took me – a white from the Christian community – to a city hospital, saw me to the casualty desk and quietly disappeared.

An hour later, with a bandage swathed around my head and some memorable bruises, I was fetched by an anxious senior colleague and retrieved my fallen scooter. I decided that I was fit for work. Later that day, I found the Indian woman in charge of the taxi that had come to my aid, and was able to give my rescuers thanks, and to return a fresh handkerchief. She graciously declined any payment for the taxi ride, or reward for herself and the other 'Good Samaritans'.

A life-changing message had been sent to me that morning: 'Welcome to the world that you have just entered and must serve in your work – a new world where kindness transcends colour, culture and creed'.

The memory of that morning's experience has moved and inspired me ever since. In a very real sense, this book began on that day. Since then, I have spent nearly thirty years studying, encountering, teaching and writing about the world's great belief- and value-systems, both religious and secular, from Australian Aboriginal to Zen and Zulu. From them and their members, I have sought insight into how to work for a world where conscience transcends colour, culture and creed and where it transforms evil into lasting good. This book is the result.

As we explore these issues, it is necessary to remember that because the book is about a new, inclusive approach to conscience, it is like doing a jigsaw puzzle. You proceed bit by bit, slowly at first, and only later do you see the full picture and how the pieces all fit together. In working towards that fuller picture, it helps to have a basic sense of the main realities of our times because they are reshaping our world context and also reshaping our understanding of conscience itself. We will return to these realities in the second last part of this chapter.

WASHINGTON, DC IN 2001

To set the global scene for what follows, I want to take readers back to Friday 14 September 2001, just a few days after the horrors of 9/11, back to a critical moment for conscience as a potentially world-transforming force. According to my media source, President George W. Bush, in the presence of Christian, Jewish and Muslim representatives, addressed the United States of America (USA) and the world from the National Cathedral in Washington, DC. In dramatic words, he declared that 'our responsibility to history is already clear: to answer these attacks and *rid the world of evil*' (Bush 2001; emphasis added).

In the months and years since then, the world has seen where this has led: to a military attack by the USA and the allies it could muster, such as Britain and Australia, on the Iraq of Saddam Hussein. As we all remember, the grounds given for this attack were Hussein's supposed possession and impending use of weapons of mass destruction, and his rumoured links with Al-Qaeda.

President Bush's speech in the National Cathedral and its practical outcome might seem to some people a triumph of goodness for the world's mightiest nation, and indeed for all who worry about evil in the world. It might seem like a noble fusion of three great forces: conscience, religion and power, and quite possibly this was the President's sincere intention. His speech, however, has been seen by many as simplistic, self-righteous and superficial and his declaration as a setback for the cause of justice and peace in the world – for conscience at its best. This book explains why. In the name of conscience as a shared human power, and not only the prerogative of the USA, the West or any other part of the planet, it issues a call to all who are anxious about the future of the planet, and especially to the rich and powerful Western world. This book suggests that there is a better way forward, a way based on the only secure foundations for a world of lasting well-being: the way of a transformed sense of good and evil, right and wrong and the values that such a moral sense includes.

Thus if President Bush could have preached peace, instead of violence, he could have avoided war in Iraq; he could have used 9/11 as an opportunity for ethical action of the kind described in this book. As the results of his choices show, the USA's action in the Middle East has not led to 'the greater good', which it could have produced.

This book explains how all human beings around the world can achieve a great leap forward in our quest for greater well-being. It points the way to a path that can prepare us for both a richer kind of national citizenship wherever we live, and especially for global citizenship in a world worth having.

GREED: THE GLOBAL CANCER

Ours is a world wracked by a new struggle on a global scale, but the struggle is not with terrorism. Nor is it against poverty, Aids or damage to the environment. Important though these and other struggles are, they are only the main arenas of a greater conflict. The real one is the struggle that must now be waged by the standard-bearers of conscience against the forces of greed and violence that are jack-booting their way to world control.

The struggle can only be won if those who are committed to the goodness of life join one another, for that is the essence of conscience – the wise and humane management of how we relate to one another, making the best of our togetherness for the benefit of all. It is the convergence in our lives of generosity, truthfulness and the kind of beautiful presence that is possible even amidst great hardship. There are many examples: South Africa's Truth and Reconciliation Commission is one, as are healthy emergency relief organisations, happy families, sports teams and workplaces where mutual support is a reality.

This book is about how the struggle can be won by the power of conscience. It is inspired by the lesson of history that moral power can be the world's most potent life-changing and world-changing event.

Was it not conscience that inspired and mobilised the genius of Abraham Lincoln, Florence Nightingale, Gandhi, Martin Luther King Jr. and Nelson Mandela, not to speak of the great religious leaders of history? Was it not conscience that gave South Africa democracy and liberation? Science itself, which some would say is humanity's greatest achievement, can be seen as the product of a relentless and often courageous passion for truth and therefore as a mountain-top of the human spirit. These achievements show that we are not being hopelessly naive when we pin our hopes on humanity's moral potential.

Mindful of the wounded state of our world after many millennia of moral effort, with its mass poverty, violence and corruption, we may well be tempted to think that conscience has failed. While we must certainly be realistic about the extent of evil in the world, and above all, about its subtle way of masquerading as good, to give up on conscience would be a dreadful mistake. The truth is very different, for at its richest and best as a worldwide source of healing and well-being, conscience – or ethical living, as some of us speak of it – is perhaps only now becoming possible because only now is the world becoming free and informed enough for a global vision of right and wrong, and for what I wish to call deep ethics, as will be seen elsewhere in this book. We will see that conscience is the world's creatively generous potential taming its destructive potential – dream prevailing over nightmare, generosity over greed.

Why then do we see signs of a moral meltdown all around us: violence, starving innocents amidst self-caused obesity, corrupt politicians, public servants, professionals and business people, insane acts of war, unethical religion and apparently irreversible damage to the natural environment?

In a booklet called *Creating the New Ethic*, Lloyd Geering has pointed to the rise of autonomy – of self-rule – as a factor (1991: 5ff.). Over the past few centuries, many societies have experienced a major movement of individuals asserting a right to question just about everything and to decide the basic issues of their lives for themselves. This is what personal autonomy means.

The great German philosopher Immanuel Kant summarised this new reality very well in the preface to his *Critique of Pure Reason*, first published in 1781, writing that 'the present age is in especial degree an age of criticism, and to criticism everything must submit' (1933: 9). The result has been widespread questioning and rejection of traditional moral authorities and principles. We see this most clearly in the emergence of a much more liberal and tolerant sexual morality in many Western countries.

The greater freedom that has come from the demand for autonomy has undoubtedly brought political and social benefits to many. But it is one thing to question and reject traditional sources of guidance in the name of personal freedom, and quite another to replace them with better values leading to increased well-being, as if those values come about without effort on our part, like the seasons. I see little sign that this challenge has been adequately faced, which is another reason for writing this book.

Other factors have also weakened the grip of traditional values. In parts of the world such as Western Europe, Australia and New Zealand, religion has waned as a guide to our sense of right and wrong. Where it remains influential, as in the USA, much of Africa and the Middle East, the influence is often authoritarian, alienating those who want reasons and evidence, not unquestioning obedience. As a result of factors such as these, we see the signs of moral decay mentioned above. What these grim realities show, however, is not the end of conscience and the humane, truth-loving lifestyles it produces. They show us that the world is outgrowing the adolescent moralities that have dominated people's lives for many centuries, giving us the moral meltdowns we see around us.

CONSCIENCE AS THE CURE

The world therefore needs a rebirth of conscience that will empower all of us, not only to rule ourselves wisely and well, but also to rule our rulers, especially the most powerful of them. Encouraging the growth of a wiser and more inclusive sense of right and wrong in the USA at this time is particularly urgent because of its global power, its way of using that power in the early years of the twenty-first century and the strident, highly conservative, intolerant kind of Christianity that has recently come to the fore in that country.

So humanity needs a new chapter in the story of conscience, to transcend the bigotries, faltering moralities and worsening problems of the present, giving us an ethic built on experience, on realism about human nature and the state of the world; built also on justified confidence in the creative potential of an informed, liberated, and committed moral sense. As will be seen, especially in Chapter Five, the central strategy of this new genesis will be to make sure that power is governed by sound values, making conscience-based living much more effective.

We are the world's future or its failure. We must choose which we will be, for in each one of us, conscience itself is on trial, particularly in those of us who have power, influence and resources. The same applies to the nations of the world, and to none more so than those with the lion's share of the world's power and wealth.

APARTHEID'S LESSON FOR THE WORLD

This book about the values needed for a future of greater well-being springs from my love of a vast and majestic land, hauntingly beautiful and richly blessed with natural resources. Long ago, it was home only to native peoples and vast herds of wildlife. Then, in the wake of a famous seafaring explorer, came settler forebears from Europe, first of all, the Dutch and the English, Bible in hands, but not afraid to use the gun when necessary, followed by others from many lands. Together they built a new nation of great prosperity and massive military power to control their world. Then a day dawned when that nation came under armed attacked by radicals who rejected everything it stood for. A new president and his people found themselves facing a fateful question: how best should they use their newly gained power?

I refer here, of course, to my own country, South Africa, doing so as a white, male ethics professor who rejoices every day at the marvel of a new, post-apartheid society in the making. But I also speak out of admiration for another, far more powerful country, the USA. I do so as one who ponders anxiously and urgently what this great nation will do with its globally unrivalled power for good or ill, as it dominates the world the way white South Africans used to dominate the southern part of Africa.

But the USA does not stand alone in today's world. At the time of writing, the USA's approach to terrorism has Britain and Australia as allies, two countries I greatly admire and have often visited. In terms of personal wealth, they match their US counterparts. Much the same holds true for New Zealand, Canada and Western Europe – and for the richest section of South Africa's people, mostly whites. But since it is only the USA that has the power to dominate the world, this country is the main focus of the discussion that follows.

Since the day I arrived at Kennedy Airport as a graduate student in August 1968, people in the USA have been very generous to me, helping to widen and deepen my mind and educate my conscience. The generosity started even earlier with the wording of the opening paragraph of this section, which closely echoes words I heard from one of the USA's finest sons, Bobby Kennedy, in a speech he gave during his South African visit to our anti-apartheid student community at the University of Cape Town on 6 June 1966. Giving me, for one, immense heart, he told us that each time a person 'stands up for an ideal, or acts to improve the lot of others, or strikes out against injustice, he sends forth a tiny ripple of hope, and crossing each other from a million different centres of energy and daring, those ripples can build a current which can sweep down the mightiest walls of oppression and resistance' (undated press report by Stanley Uys). The benefits I have received from people in the USA have continued down the years, as I will show in various places in this book.

Especially since 9/11, alas, the USA and its allies' actions have become highly problematic for the future stability and prosperity of the world because these actions are not ending terrorism, but refuelling it. The mid-2006 conflict between Israel and Lebanon and the news of a plot hatched in Britain to blow up airliners en route to the USA, strike many of us as the proof of this conviction. Thus, the USA and its allies face a challenge that has much in common with the one that we, the former overlords of South Africa, faced in the apartheid period of our history that ended in 1994. Under apartheid a rich, heavily armed, mostly white and largely Christian minority sought to impose its will by force on a dark-skinned, poor and ill-armed majority. And this minority believed that it held the moral high ground, seeing itself as a civilising force for good.

So I want to return the generosity I have experienced in the USA, Britain, Australia and other parts of the wealthy world, to speak about some of the lessons I have learnt both in South Africa and in those countries concerning the values that must underlie a world of lasting well-being, lessons of heart and soul about how and why unchallenged power corrupts, while shared power transforms and liberates.

To make my point as forcefully as possible, I want to examine what is meant by 'the apartheid world'. At the 2001 World Summit on

Sustainable Development, South Africa's President Thabo Mbeki used this label, and brought it into the wider world's vocabulary of injustice. Neither the words nor the idea are new, for many of us had already come to think of the deeply unjust state of the planet in these terms. But none of us can command global media attention the way that President Mbeki did. This makes his utterance very important in getting people of conscience the world over, and especially in the USA, to get real about the state of the earth and their responsibility for it.

What does it mean to think of our planet as the apartheid world? Was Mbeki simply using a highly provocative and challenging expression, or is there a deeper message encoded in that expression? Not being privy to his intentions, I have no idea of the answer. But I do have questions and ideas of my own on the subject, and mostly they have to do with the ethics of power.

Power without conscience is tyranny. If the twentieth century, with its Hitlers, Stalins, Pol Pots and Chairman Maos taught us any ethical lesson, surely, this is it. South Africans know this better than most from their own experience of apartheid, in which power also broke free of conscience and became nothing less than tyranny. The apartheid state, with its huge gaps between the wealthy and the poor, the educated and the educationally deprived, the healthy and the diseased, was the direct result of an oppressive control of power on the part of many of the white people, who did not see it for the gross injustice it was. We also know that apartheid was a human construct, like all other tyrannies, and not a brute fact of nature like the cycle of the seasons or continental drift. It grew out of decisions and choices, and out of the defective consciences of those with the greatest power.

In other words, apartheid didn't just happen. It was *made* to happen, and now it is being unmade. It was evil and its evil is now slowly being replaced by something better, no matter how far South Africans may still be from achieving the common good for which all decent people yearn. This reality prompts me to suspect that President Mbeki was making exactly the same point about global apartheid, namely that it carries a terrible moral price and that the account must be delivered to those who have run up this worst of global debts, namely the rich and powerful.

But there is more to decode. Living on an apartheid planet means that those in the so-called developed world with the oppressive power, wealth and resources are like the whites of the old South Africa, and indeed, many in the new one. They, or rather we, for I am one of them, are the beneficiaries and perpetuators of global injustice, whose victims are the people of the global South and the worldwide natural environment that we plunder. We are the ones whose consciences, and at times religions, sit easily with the unjust privileges we give ourselves, often gained through violence against others. Could this also have been on President Mbeki's mind?

Within the apartheid elite of the old South Africa, there was a super-elite. In terms of wealth, it was dominated by English-speaking whites, especially in the early days of white domination. But in terms of the real, day-to-day power of politics and military muscle, that super-elite was of course the country's old National Party, with its control ranging from broadcasting and legislation to outright, murderous brutality, and with its complete and utter disdain for the views and values of those who disagreed with it.

The term 'global apartheid' therefore has a further meaning, namely the oppressive presence of a global super-elite, whether or not this part of what President Mbeki was meaning. And does this not imply that today the ethical spotlight of the world's conscience must be directed mainly at the section of the USA that sees itself as the citadel of goodness, supports the war in the Middle East and seems determined to have its own way, no matter what the rest of the world says, if needs be at gunpoint – simply because of its unmatched power and wealth? Has this powerful sector of a great and essentially honourable nation become the National Party of global apartheid?

In global terms, is the planet now where South Africa was not so long ago, sinking into a deadly, global state of emergency under the 'bosses' of an apartheid world? Being both diplomatic and courteous, President Mbeki was not, of course, insinuating such an unflattering comparison. But the rest of us can and must ask these questions. A leader is not made morally sound merely by seeming sincere and calling other nations evil, but by humane wisdom. Is this what the world is seeing from those who wield the world's great armed power these days?

Or could President Mbeki perhaps have been sending a different message altogether? Could he have been sending out a message of hope rather than judgement, reminding the majority of the world's poor and powerless that just as South African apartheid could be beaten, and was, so too can global apartheid be beaten, and surely will be, and that those in the rich and heartless world who now maintain it will also be unseated, just as the once-mighty and well-heeled overlords of apartheid have been dethroned?

These are the hard truths to which President Mbeki's words inexorably lead, whatever he may have meant. This is the lesson that the rich and powerful Western world can learn from South Africa's experience of what happens when conscience is neither deep, nor all embracing, and when power breaks free from moral control.

Central to this lesson is that sincerity and a strong religious faith are not enough to prevent the corrupting tendencies of dominant power. We, the overlords of racist South Africa, for all our regular churchgoing and Bible-reading, were blind to our own blindness until others, in particular, the black people of our country, gave us the gift of a vastly enhanced moral vision. We could not truly see that we too, well-to-do though we were, had become victims, that evil is not only the gross ugliness of vulgar racists and bullies, it also has a way of poisoning the self-righteous and their deeds.

Domination cuts us off from truths we all need if we are to be truly free. It confines us to the company of those who think, value and act as we do, removing us from others who see vital truths about us, including our shortcomings, our unjustified self-confidence and self-righteousness and particularly, the subtle evils that invade the souls of those given to a passion for power over others.

What has liberated people like me from the captivity we didn't even realise we were suffering is the courage, truth and generosity of others who understood that a worthwhile future can only be built if we build it as partners and never at gunpoint, that it can only come from conscience, not muscle – like those two Indian South Africans who helped me all those years ago when we white South Africans rode roughshod over people like them.

But for conscience to free people and empower them, it cannot remain silent. It needs its great ally, the power of the truth-bearing word. Such is the passionate conviction that has driven the long journey that has led to the writing of this book. It offers practical resources of heart, mind and hands to those who feel a deep disquiet at the state of the world and are open to creative ways of responding. It charts a way that they can follow for themselves to become more than simply ethically committed national citizens, a way to become global ethical citizens.

A PLEA TO THE USA AND ITS ALLIES

To the USA especially, but also to other rich countries such as Britain and Australia, this book therefore sends an urgent plea: you alone have the economic and military power to reshape the entire world for generations to come. Will the world continue to be a divided place of exploitation, conflict and misunderstanding, or will it become a more humane, just, peaceful and prosperous planet? Will the USA be seen as the world's loved and admired bigger brother, or as a ruthless, greedy bully?

My times in the USA make me sure that its people want to be the world's friend and benefactor, but they also make me, as one who has lived through the stunning recent changes in my own country, call on citizens of the USA, especially those who sense the need for greater justice, care and concern in the way their nation uses its power, to make their sense of right and wrong and the actions it triggers as deep and wide, as it is sincere.

So I call on them (and indeed on all people of good will) to be passionate about more than family values and national interests, and to enlarge the circle of their active concern in order to influence the world, not as a superpower, but as a 'super-friend'. I appeal to them to draw on the finest values in their religions, but at the same time to accept that all faiths and philosophies must help enrich the world's conscience. As the motherland of modern democracy, I urge the USA and other democrats everywhere to maximise the potential of that system of shared power to be a truly world-transforming force that cannot be imposed, and to lead by example and service, not by domination. 'Help us all build a global ethic together as equals' is the message of conscience to them, 'or neither you, nor any of us, will experience a future of greater security and well-being where the fires of terrorist rage have finally been extinguished'.

In working for the good, we will stumble, sometimes badly. Many of us around the world think that the USA is stumbling at this time. Significant numbers of Britons and Australians are deeply concerned about the ravenous consumer culture that is present in their own countries. Many in South Africa think that our own country has stumbled badly over the HIV/Aids pandemic and over the tyranny that is doing such appalling damage to Zimbabwe at this time. However, this is not the point, for in a world where freedom is real and the dark side of our natures is also real, no outcome is guaranteed in the quest for a better future. Mistakes will be made. So long as we learn from them, keep working on our values, and are genuinely committed to the greater, common good, they need not be anything worse than temporary setbacks in the long, global struggle for a better world, even though many of them involve great loss and pain at a personal level for those afflicted.

The point therefore is to strive again and again to be the best we can, encouraged by the fact that we are all equipped with the potential for good, a potential that will be explored in the next chapter. As will also be seen in the next chapter, there are rich resources of conscience in the world around us, and ours is a time of unprecedented opportunity for the forces of generosity and integrity, as I will explain later in this chapter. We must also face up to the wrong we sometimes do, at times in the name of good, make changes and become transformed. But this takes more than personal moral courage. It takes the gift of support from those around us, as I will show now from my own experience, for in the domain of conscience, you can't go it alone.

SAVED BY KINDNESS AND A CLANGER

One of my own most important lessons of growth through the supportiveness of others happened very early and very embarrassingly in my time at what is now called the Episcopal Divinity School in Cambridge, Massachusetts. It took place in the autumn of 1968. I was in the USA on an international scholarship awarded by the School – itself a wonderful example of the generosity the USA is capable of – after studying theology in South Africa and at Oxford.

I counted myself a committed opponent of apartheid, but despite my good intentions, political views, friendships with black South Africans and excellent education, I was quite unaware that the racist context of white South Africa had nastily infected a key part of my own life – my vocabulary.

This is what happened. I had signed up for a course on group dynamics, wanting to enhance my interpersonal skills. The course more than met my expectations, but what was truly liberating for me happened informally in one of the first class meetings. We were discussing behaviours that are bad for harmonious personal relationships, as I recall, and I suddenly felt that I could put my finger on the problem. I think I was correct about it – that groups suffer when a few individuals try to dominate and talk too much – but what was terrible was how I expressed it. Completely blind to its utter offensiveness, I used a phrase that must have entered my vocabulary in my junior school days in white

South Africa, for it was certainly never part of the way things were said in my home. I called the problem 'the nigger in the woodpile'.

There was a loud gasp in the room and everybody's eyes widened with shock at what I had said. I vividly recall my immediate feeling of confusion at their reaction, and then almost at once, the terrible truth hit me. I dropped my head in shame, turned scarlet (or so my burning cheeks felt), and blurted out my abject apology.

Then, from the kindness and goodness of the group, came a healing and transforming moment. They had every right to shake their heads in strong reproof and disbelief, or even to signal with their body language: what else was to be expected from a white South African? But they didn't. Instead, they all burst out laughing, grasping intuitively the truth of the situation, sensing that I had manifested blindness and naivety rather than racism and deliberately offensive speech.

Their friendly laughter and understanding were a gift of healing and growth for my sense of shame at that lapse, but also, perhaps more importantly, carried deeper truths into my life, the ethical truths that supportiveness is far more effective than condemnation in fostering personal growth, and that we all need help to find and cure the ills in our own souls. As I said above, in the world of conscience, we are not alone. How remarkable that it should be the USA, with its exceptionally strong individualism that stamped that truth so permanently into my soul.

Turning now from the personal to the global, the world around us with its mass poverty, terrorism, oppression and environmental damage is an affront to conscience. The new beginning it needs must be based on a new way to mobilise the power of commitment to others. We have had our first genesis – the genesis of our innocence, naked in 'Eden', as people familiar with the Jewish and Christian scriptures might say when thinking of our human beginnings. Now, as a global civilisation begins to be possible for the first time on this planet, we need our second genesis through the coming of a world of lasting well-being for all.

To continue with the same biblical imagery, when we lost our first Eden, it was our murdered brother's blood that cried out to us from the earth. Now it is also our mothers' blood, our sisters', our children's, our fathers', our animals' and the very life of nature itself. All of them cry out for justice, for a new genesis.

Welcome, then, to the frontier world of a new age of conscience and well-being. Behind us lie the known lands of our past, with their many physical and emotional comforts, but also their dreadful mistakes and problems. Ahead lie the beckoning territories of the future we must share with others whose ways are strange and at times even threatening to our own.

But this time we are not at the fringe of that unknown space in order to conquer it like the pioneer whites of the USA's legendary Wild West, six-guns in hand, or the Europeans who invaded South Africa, Australia and many other lands, or the army of George W. Bush smashing its way into Iraq. We are here to befriend it. It takes a special kind of person to ride out into that new dawn, a person with vision, courage and a very large heart, a pioneer in the best sense of that word. We can all be that kind of person.

A QUICK GUIDE TO CONSCIENCE

The journey that humanity as a whole must make to a world of greater well-being for all – to our new beginning – starts with a fresh understanding of what it means to live in the power of conscience and therefore on the basis of healthy, ethical values. This new understanding must be reached on the basis of an essential rule: *morality or ethics as something lived must itself be ethical and must renew itself ethically*. Later in this book, it will be seen what this involves in some detail, but for now it is enough to identify what I have come to see as the heart of the matter, in the form of simple but profound principles. Having a conscience – or living by what is right and good – means showing:

- active concern for the lasting well-being of whoever and whatever we affect, and
- active concern for ourselves individually and the future selves we could all be.
- It also means having personal integrity, and
- practising the specific values that conscience requires.

Conscience is the inner voice of ethics, of right and wrong, of good and evil. We can think of it as our built-in guidance system in the search for the good life. It is the uncomfortable feeling we get, or should get, when we tell a lie, speak cruelly, cheat on somebody, use our fists, double-park, break a promise, or do any of the many things we know are wrong. It is also the warm and noble feeling that comes when we do the right thing – standing up for a friend, being true to a team-mate, or to a partner at home, or in business, giving time, effort and money to those in need, or insisting on the truth, especially when it costs us something to do these things.

Culture is thus an essential part of conscience. But it is also the source of some great and troubling differences about what exactly is right and wrong. One culture induces suicide bombers to blow other people up as a sacred duty. Another culture dismisses those bombers as evil terrorists. This reality is why it is so vital for the world to find its way to a *shared*, global ethic, which could let us transcend such terrible divisions. I will return to this problem of divided identities, loyalties and values towards the end of Chapter Four.

This view of conscience and the arguments I shall give to support it may sound new to many readers, but it rests on a very conventional definition of ethics, a word with two meanings, according to the 1998 edition of the *New Oxford Dictionary of English*. The first meaning listed refers to human behaviour, to the world of values, decisions and actions and is usually used as a plural ('what are your ethics?'). The second meaning is mostly used as a singular ('ethics is . . .') and is greatly loved by academics like me. It refers to a field of study mostly conducted by philosophers and theologians. Sometimes it is also called moral philosophy or moral theology.

This book is chiefly about the former meaning. It is about character, conduct and cultures shaped and directed by an understanding of, a firm belief in, and a commitment to what is right and good and against what is wrong and at times even evil. It is about what the US ethicist Rushworth M. Kidder calls 'ethical fitness' (2005: 44ff.) and what I like to call an active, committed conscience.

When such an orientation to life is consciously chosen in a free and informed way, then life achieves a depth and power that can be world changing, as we see in Gandhi, Mandela, or Martin Luther King Jr. This is not to belittle the value of what we might call a habitual ethic, an ethic that results from training, starting in infancy, into habits of genuine kindness and truthfulness. An ingrained sense of right and wrong like this does not usually involve an experience of conscious commitment to a life of generosity and truthfulness. Human goodness has a range of modes from the childlike and the obedient to that of well-informed, wise and freely committed ethical icons such as those mentioned above.

Understood in this practical, real-life way, conscience, or morality, as it is also called, is a matter of wise and sound valuing, which shows itself in what we do and in the concepts we use to express it, achieving its greatest power when a caring heart and truthful lips fuse with a deep and well-informed understanding and deliberate choice.

Academics like me often go wrong here. All too often, our work on ethics is very long on theory, but short on contact with the world of experience out there. All too often, our work emphasises analysis and abstraction rather than practical application, as a few hours checking the contents of the leading academic journals in ethics over the past decade or two will show clearly.

Because we are trained to use concepts, academics often assume that ethics is primarily philosophical or theoretical, but it isn't. It is primarily a matter of valuing and doing. Clear, logical thinking and arguing can greatly enrich the processes of valuing and doing, but can never displace them from the heartland of conscience. So we have reached a situation where those of us who work in universities either make academic ethics more practical and relevant, or we condemn it to increasing irrelevance.

The definitions of conscience, ethics and morality given earlier in this section include the word 'good', so it too needs to be clarified. In general, words such as 'good' or 'goodness' stand for whatever we judge approvingly, like a good meal, painting, dog or friend. Among the great many things that we approve of, there is a set that shares a most important feature. This is the ability to bring benefit, especially to others, and since we cannot do this successfully without understanding them, their situations and needs, a concern for truth and knowledge is part of beneficial living. Goodness of this special kind is therefore present in actions that we believe will bring about some kind of genuine benefit. Of special importance are all the benefits of promoting survival, fulfilment and the deepest, most durable well-being for as many as possible.

Well-being is the central concept of this book, but what exactly does it involve? What are the values that go with this core principle? How can we identify them? Why should we understand conscience, ethics and morality as the enhancement of well-being – which is not the same as pleasure, especially mere physical pleasure – for as many as possible, and ideally for all? How does ethical living in the world of the twenty-first century differ from ethical living a century or even a generation ago? This book provides answers to those vital questions, dealing with the 'why?', the 'what?', and the 'how?' of conscience in a globalising world and showing that conscience in practice means acting in ways that let us enjoy greater well-being in the only way that is both deeply enriching and sustainable – *together!*

'Together' is a key word for conscience, ranging from any two of us to the entire, globalising planet, a planet where communication systems, market forces, pollution, the price of oil, spy satellites and the military might of the USA span and affect the globe.

This new reality leads me to a vitally important additional point about conscience: it has two focal meanings. The first is the one we all think of: the personal sense of right and wrong that we have as individuals and that defines our characters. The other one tends to be overlooked by many experts, yet it is just as important and maybe even more so. I shall call it 'context', meaning all the environments we are part of, involving other people, our organisations, cultures, nations and nature itself. As I will explain elsewhere in this book, a world of greater well-being cannot be achieved unless the transforming power of conscience also transforms the contexts in which we live. They then become hugely important supports for our efforts as individuals to live generous, truthful lives. In other words, *conscience includes both character and context.*

FORCES RESHAPING THE WORLD AND OUR VALUES

The world of the twenty-first century is, in some extremely important ways, a very different place from the world of the past. We must now note the main changes because of the major impact they have on all of us, and on how we can best strengthen our moral fibre. Seven changes stand out as especially powerful.

Democracy

The first change is democracy, which I see as involving three shifts of power from the older politics of autocratic kings and queens: downward, sideways and especially inward. We pay far too little attention to this third yet vital shift, so I will emphasise it most, after briefly commenting on the other two.

Where political power once lay in the hands of small, mostly male elites, democracy gives power to ordinary people – that is obviously the 'downward' movement of power. The sideways movement means that power rests equally with *all* people. Notice that equality is thus a key value in democracy. While most of us know this, few of us recognise the revolutionary consequences that a belief in basic human equality has for conscience and ethics. It means that primary responsibility for values such as integrity, compassion and responsibility rests with all of us as ordinary, equal citizens. Equality means that we must get beyond the trap of dependency and the calls for obedience to supposed moral authorities that goes with it, like deferring to the rulings of religious or political leaders and sacred writings simply because they say we must. If their authority is genuine, thinking, responsible people of conscience will recognise their worth and respect them for their inherent value.

This does not mean disregarding traditional moral authorities, but it does mean that we can't pass the buck to them. It stops with us. And it certainly does not mean blind obedience, or superficial use, such as uncritically believing that displaying the Ten Commandments in our multicultural schools will do much to further the cause of moral living.

The third shift is therefore the most important for conscience – the shift of power inward into the understanding and choices of each individual. Power without conscience is a terrible curse, as we saw under apartheid and other oppressive regimes, such as those of Hussein, Hitler and Stalin. For democracy to work best, the power it places in our hands must be power governed by conscience. This is one reason why each of us needs to work at the personal moral fitness that democracy needs if it is to work really well, making it much better informed and much more inclusive.

Here too, people like me who care greatly about the USA believe that the need for a transformed morality is great. What we are hearing from the White House and its supporters in the early years of the twenty-first century sounds like a narrowly nationalist ethic fed by a narrowly conservative version of traditional Protestant Christian morality, at a time when we all need to look outwards and commit ourselves and our powers to the greatest possible inclusivity.

The spread of democracy is the most significant political reality of our time. It is also an ethical achievement of the highest order, incomplete though it is, even in a country such as the USA. In that great country, otherwise admiring visitors such as myself, find much less knowledge of the wider world than in any other developed society. This is cause for very real concern, the point being that democracy does best not only where there is liberty, but also where knowledge levels are high and where the understanding of the global human condition is both broad and deep. Cultural insularity works strongly against that requirement, besides making unwise decisions and policies more likely, as apartheid South Africa learnt to its detriment during its years of isolation. This is partly why I reacted with dismay at the words of President George W. Bush in the National Cathedral a few days after 9/11. While I sensed in those words real sincerity, I also sensed serious cultural and ethical narrowness, a limitation that works strongly against a global ethic worthy of the name.

Embedded in the democratic way of using power are some vital values such as equality, fairness, inclusiveness, constrained personal freedom (which allows each of us to be as free as possible, as long as the same is possible for everybody else and nobody gets hurt) and what we might call provisionality. This means never allowing any individual, leader, party or policy to have absolute status and immunity to change, for the simple reason that we humans and all our structures are fallible – perhaps mostly when we believe that we speak for an infallible God.

Nonetheless, even an incomplete democracy is a vast improvement over the inequalities and injustices of traditional monarchs and dictators. The emergence in recent centuries of the human rights movement is a related gain for the forces of conscience because it protects individuals from the vastly greater powers of governments, the state, large organisations and even collections of fellow citizens. However, it is also very incomplete because of too much emphasis on individual rights and too little on the moral responsibility that makes rights possible in the first place, quite apart from the ongoing plight of women, children, animals and the environment being dominated by those who wield power, most of whom are, of course, men, in many parts of the world.

Overall, the political dimension of the world of the early twenty-first century is thus a mixed bag, with important moral gains as well as worrisome moral problems. I think this means that we have an opportunity to build on what has been gained and transform what remains wrong in the politics of the world, chiefly its surviving despots and absolute monarchs and the incomplete versions of democracies in what used to be called 'the free world'. I also think that we must start with ourselves because the only people who can transform ethically defective political, economic, religious and educational structures are ethically transformed people, which is why I see democracy's inward shift of power as the key to the flourishing of democracy overall.

Cultural diversity

Experiencing a rich array of cultures as a daily reality is the second factor that has changed life for us and is now challenging conscience itself to stop being insular. It was well summarised in a lecture I heard in 1982 by the late Ninian Smart, who did so much to make the study of the world's religions a rigorous academic subject (Smart 1973). He spoke of cultural diversity in that lecture as represented by the London bus-driver with a shamrock in his turban. While there are many parts of the world where cultural uniformity still lingers, for most of us, those days are over in response to the discovery that many indeed are the ways of being worthily human.

In former times, everybody in a given society would be English, Zulu, Islamic or Roman Catholic, with little or even no real contact with people belonging to other cultures, faiths and beliefs because those cultures mostly existed in isolation from others. This is why the Bible, for example, makes no reference to Buddhism or Chinese culture, and vice versa. This situation has gone forever in most parts of the world. Different cultures now exist side by side and in daily contact – each of them with their own approach to conscience.

Most us, however, remain largely ignorant of those other paths to goodness. Some of us think they are inferior to our ways. If we are to harness the power of conscience as a worldwide force, we must do so in a way that reflects this diversity and respond to it with respect, and with an openness to moral value wherever it can be found. This entire book is based on such an inclusive approach and in Chapter Four, it is used in order to sketch an outline of a moral map of the planet's great value-systems.

The lordship of the market
The third of these world-changing forces is the unfettered domination – if neoliberal economics continues to have its way – of the market as the 'Grand Narrative' or controlling myth of our time. The Nazi myth of a superior Aryan race destined by history to dominate other peoples is a good example of a grand narrative and its dangerous power. So is the white South African myth of the whites having a God-given Christian mission to convert and civilise darkest Africa.

In a neoliberal economic reality, we encounter the notion that the market is what history inevitably leads to in the drive to put a price on everything, a drive that is approaching the status of a new sacred cow. It is important to grasp that in this doctrine, the market is lord and master and leaves no space for real freedom in how we create and use wealth, a notion perfectly captured in a phrase Margaret Thatcher reputedly liked to use: 'There is no alternative'.

Putting a price on everything in a world as unevenly resourced as ours naturally means making many goods and services unaffordable to many. This is why we also encounter the lordship of the market as a growing gap between rich and poor, and as a growing mix of hopelessness, rage and violent reaction among the latter, as the affluent sector flaunts images of its self-indulgence, while relentlessly with-holding enjoyment of life's pleasures from the poor – except, of course, by the recourse of the poor to what the rich call theft.

Science and technology
Everybody knows that science and technology have radically changed the world. Less well known is their impact on both our practice and understanding of conscience, as I know from several years of developing and teaching a university course on science and ethics.

A passion for truth is one of the hallmarks of moral strength. As our most reliable and inclusive way of discovering the truth about the world and our own bodies, science is clearly an outstanding ethical achievement, quite apart from the light it sheds on many of the moral problems confronting us today, such as stem cell research, cloning, genetic modification and abortion. And who would doubt that such fruits of science as the best discoveries in medical and agricultural technology could offer us massive benefits?

But there are also serious ethical problems. Just as democracy requires conscience if it is truly to serve society, so too do science and technology. Most of us know about the horrific abuse of these two mighty forces of the modern world in places such as Hitler's Germany. Scientists and engineers there created the technologies of mass extermination. In our own time, there are grave worries about scientists in the service of powerful corporations running amok in the genetic modifications of organisms.

The best way to prevent atrocities like the Nazi abuse of science and technology from happening again, or genetics becoming a curse, is to ensure that science is governed by conscience, not by greed or hatred. This is another reason for working at our moral fitness. Science is already a global reality, and its inherent moral worth and potential are vital resources for a better world, provided that our scientists and those who fund them are governed by a strong, well-informed, and above all, globally shared sense of right and wrong. Brain science is also already enlarging our understanding of the way conscience works, as I will show in Chapter Two, when exploring the workings of human nature.

Religion: Blessing and curse

Nor is all well on the spiritual front, especially with traditional, institutional religion, the next of the great contemporary realities affecting ethics. Nobody would deny the great good that often flows from deep religious commitment. But the fact remains that our religions have divided the world, at times murderously. Furthermore, they give us different, and at times contradictory, teachings about the nature of reality and the basis of human goodness. This, alas, fragments and weakens the world's conscience at a time when it needs a strong, united sense of right and wrong more than ever.

However, the various faiths share certain core values such as love, compassion, truthfulness, justice and sexual decency, giving the world an important but still insufficient basis for a global ethic. It will be seen later in this book just how valuable this positive side of religion is. It will also be seen how some of our faith-based value-systems are hampering moral growth in a globalising world, none more so than the highly conservative ones in the USA because of their influence on its leaders, or in parts of the Muslim world where some radicals seem ever ready to defend God with the gun, despite the Qur'an's beautiful vision of divine compassion, and in aspects of Israeli life that show none of the magnificent loving-kindness called for in the Hebrew Bible.

Through a man like George W. Bush, a sincere but ethically problematic, divisive and conservative version of Christian morality is now impacting on the entire world, with deeply disturbing results because it is not spreading democracy and decency but distrust, distress and even disgust, not among scoundrels such as Saddam Hussein, but among good and decent people. The damage to the movement for a global conscience could hardly be worse.

Secularisation, de-secularisation and identity

The sixth trend is a paradoxical one. Part of it is secularisation, which comes about when, to a greater or lesser extent, the controlling hand of traditional kinds of religion over society and over individuals declines and in some cases even disappears. Secularised people claim the right to make up their own minds and reach their own decisions independently of, and sometimes against, institutional religious teaching and values.

This trend is mostly evident in the West. We see it especially in politics, government and education. It also affects our view of the role of religion in society by encouraging us to be tolerant towards all systems of belief, with equal status for them all in all public spaces. And it means that people who hold no religious beliefs of the traditional kind at all enjoy the same equality and tolerance, and so too, do those who reject all religion. If we are to rebuild conscience in morally sensitive ways, we must include this new reality, not ignore or dismiss it. People with no religion are just as much part of the commonwealth of conscience as believers are.

But now a reverse trend is discernible in the form of de-secularisation. This is the resurgence of conservative and fundamentalist forms of religion. We are all aware of its power in parts of the Muslim world, but what concerns me much more is its growth in countries of the West, especially the USA, because it represents a return to the obedience mode that I judge to be very damaging to human maturity, coupled with a dangerously simplistic two-value ethic: good versus evil, us versus them. The effect is to make the quest for good into a battlefield, and other people into our enemies. That such an outlook runs directly counter to the inclusive approach to conscience that I am proposing, should be very clear. It hardens our differences by emphasising different and even hostile identities. Many born-again Christians, hardline young Muslims and belligerent Zionists in Israel's West Bank see themselves as having little or nothing important in common with what they think of as outsiders, a trend that is bad news for the creation of a united human conscience.

As a countermeasure, I therefore give some suggestions in Chapter Three about how people can retain the identities that their creeds and cultures give them, while also coming to see others not as outsiders or enemies, but as fellow members of the global human community and as potential sources of an enriched sense of personal identity.

Mass poverty amidst wealth for the few

Far less impressive for people with caring souls than the gains made in democratic politics and by the human rights movement is the world's economic dimension, the seventh of the forces I see as especially powerful in changing our world and challenging our conscience. Our world is disfigured by hideous, mass poverty on one hand, and vast wealth for a lucky, and at times, ruthlessly greedy minority on the other. It is further disfigured by damage to the natural environment and is being gravely harmed by the kind of neoliberal economic system that so wantonly rewards self-interest. A prime example is the kind of business that recruits and retains its chief executive officer by means of a salary package a thousand times higher than that of ordinary staff members, or pays its executives performance bonuses, even when the business reports a financial loss.

As one who was born and bred in Africa, even in relatively well-off South Africa, I experience the widening gap between the rich and the poor as especially painful. Here, more than anywhere else, the world situation is an insult to conscience and a shameful indictment of the so-called moral sense of the rich world, with its worsening syndromes of self-inflicted obesity, wastefulness and indifference.

Poverty is, of course, no newcomer to the world. However, what is new is an ethically disturbing trend that seems to have been gathering momentum since the collapse of communism and the resultant rise of global capitalism. In his book *The Super-Rich*, Stephen Haseler points out that while this new economic reality has witnessed a sharp increase in the ranks and vast wealth of a relatively few people, it has also witnessed a worsening problem of global poverty and a weakening of the middle-income group (2000: 1–26). While few of us regret the coming of freedom to communist countries that had none until 1989, with the end of the Cold War, nobody with a conscience can take comfort from the grim reality of fabulous wealth for a few amidst poverty and destitution for many. There must be a better way to run the world economy than this.

SOURCES OF A GLOBAL ETHIC

It is thus very clear that the world needs a renewed, shared quest for greater well-being, based on a renewed conscience, a renewed ethic, that is effective both locally and globally. On what can we base such an ethic? This book is based on five sources:

- Firstly, on our shared humanity. We must ask what our personal experience in our particular culture reveals about ourselves, our values, and our motivations. What is perhaps most novel about the approach to conscience in this book is precisely the use of ordinary human experience, for reasons that are explained in Chapter Two.
- Secondly, I draw on the common core of sound, long-standing values in the world's religious faiths. I do so because of their vast influence over very many centuries, which does not mean being blind to the evils that some believers have inflicted on others, nor does it mean being blind to the good brought about by secularised people.
- Thirdly, I make use of science, especially as it helps us to understand our human nature, our moral sense and the cosmos of which we are part.
- My fourth source is the logical power of reason, in order to proceed as logically as possible as I build my case for conscience as the passport to a world of greater well-being.
- Finally, I draw on the evidence of the actual practice of the ethic that takes shape when we draw on the other four sources.

two

Self-Knowledge — The Clue to Conscience

The scene is a small conference room at a city hotel. A dozen professional men and women from different cultural backgrounds and creeds sit at a U-shaped table, waiting for an ethics workshop to begin. The speaker greets them, pauses a moment, and then surprises them by asking this question: 'What do you want most from life for yourself and those you care about, and what do you want least for yourself, and for them?'

Answers begin to flow and the speaker notes them on a flip-chart. It is his way of starting the journey that they will make in the workshop into the deeper meanings of good and evil. It is also the way that this book takes readers into the same journey, a starting point that can make us more aware of ourselves primarily as human beings, rather than as South Africans, US citizens, Britons or any of our other unshared identities.

On what can the world's people with their different cultures build a united sense of right and wrong? As this book calls for something our planet urgently needs, but does not yet have, an enriched, enlarged, deepened, effective and above all, shared conscience, it must be created *together*. This calls for a process that is open to anybody, anywhere, and that does not depend on our cultures and creeds because they separate us. My method is to turn to something that we do share: human nature itself, approached in a way that is open to anybody. This approach suggests that we need to turn inward, thinking deeply and carefully about our own experience, and what it shows about the depths of our beings.

From this point, I move to something else we all share: our membership of the wider world outside of ourselves. We can think of this as a journey of both self-discovery and world-discovery. It brings to light three vital realities about human nature and the wider world: that we humans share a drive for the greatest well-being; that our creativity includes the power to transform conscience itself; and that we are part and parcel of a seamless, interconnected wider world and cosmos. It also shows that these three realities mean that as beings equipped by nature for real, effective freedom of choice, we can be deeply ethical beings who must decide what to value most and live accordingly.

I shall tell how I have made this journey of self-discovery and how I encourage others to make it for themselves in four steps, by returning to the workshop described in the opening sentences of this chapter.

WHAT WE WANT MOST

Over the past decade of my active work on issues of conscience, I have begun most of my workshops by asking the audience the question at the beginning of this chapter about what they want most to experience and what they want most to avoid. This serves a double purpose. Firstly, it gets everybody involved right from the start. Doing so gives life to the policy of treating conscience as a shared project and not the exclusive domain of the guru, and takes us firmly away from the obedience mode that I find such a problem for moral growth. And secondly, it puts vital information on the table, as will be seen later in this chapter.

Books can travel much further and reach many more people than their authors' spoken words. So I want to invite readers to answer these questions for themselves, in order to extend the exercise to other contexts and situations. All of us can do what Mahatma Gandhi pioneered in the 21 formative years he spent in South Africa, namely, to make our own lives a great experiment with values, words I am taking from the title of his famous work, *An Autobiography or The Story of my Experiments with Truth* (1990). However, I must emphasise that this first step of focusing on what people want and don't want is only a starting point. It is not by any means the whole process. Important though our desires are, much more is involved in living by the power of conscience, as will be seen in the section on well-being later in this chapter.

My audiences have ranged from sports coaches and their players to busy professionals and questing religious believers, and from executives to students. They have included people from a variety of cultures: African, Christian, Muslim, Hindu, Jewish, secularist and others, with a balance of both genders and all ages. While this is by no means a worldwide representative sample, neither does it reflect only one culture.

South Africa, where these sessions have taken place, is a very significant place to do such work. This is firstly because of the country's unusually long-standing heritage of cultural diversity. People of African, European, Malaysian and South Asian descent have lived in South Africa for far longer than in most other countries. There is also the vicious, tragic reality of our past and the cultural separation that was enforced under apartheid. As most people around the world know, massive efforts were made over a very long period to keep people of different colours, languages, faiths and cultures apart and in great ignorance of one another.

Mercifully, that hateful piece of social control is now over, but its effects have not yet vanished. Apartheid's supporters argued that human differences, both those we are born with, and those we learn, are more powerful than any similarities. This led them to believe that people of different races had to be kept separate, by force if necessary, allegedly for their own good. A country where the whole of society was relentlessly organised on this basis, until little more than a decade ago, is therefore a very revealing place to look for evidence of the contrary: for a shared human nature that is deeper in us than any of our differences, even those we are born with, and deeper than any sense of basic difference hammered into us by apartheid or any other ideology, such as nationalism.

To return now to those workshops of mine, always the answers to my question are essentially the same: the participants want survival, health, happiness, success, respect, wealth, friendship, pleasure, safety, love, esteem, beauty, and so on. With a bit of prodding by me, the two most famous three-letter words in the English language are added: God and sex, the former standing for a desire for meaning and value in life, rather than simply for a personal deity. The lists are not identical but the same core desires come up again and again, as do the same core aversions: failure, accident, pain, tragedy, bereavement, fear, poverty, rejection, violence, illness and the like. My own experience is the same: I want the same good things and also want to be spared their opposites.

Encouraged by the sameness of answers from these South African groups and related discussions in the USA, Britain, Australia, and New Zealand, and encouraged by what I hear about genetics to believe that there is such a thing as a shared human nature (though not one that imprisons us) I want to propose that the same pattern of answers would emerge anywhere on earth. We may smile or laugh or cry at different things, but we all smile, laugh and cry, and we all seem to know what these facial expressions and sounds mean.

Having put together a list of about a dozen main desires and aversions, my next move is to point out that some of the things we want most (self-preservation, love, health or happiness), or reject most strongly (pain or misery), are not matters of choice or education. My workshop participants and I agree that we simply find ourselves made in such a way as to want them, or shy away from them. We find that we are like this *by nature* – the word 'nature' meaning that which is inborn and cannot be changed by our will-power. Other values, such as a love of poetry, sport and music, or a fear of spiders (but apparently not of falling) are acquired and can be changed. Any proposed way of living that hopes to work in practice must take account of this distinction, adapting itself to what cannot be changed in us and working creatively with what can.

The preceding paragraphs contend that we human beings share a desire for very similar kinds of enjoyable, fulfilling experiences. Now it is necessary to extend and defend this view of what we all want most into a discussion of several important terms and issues: values, the role of feelings, well-being, maximising well-being, brain science, and the history of conscience.

Values

This clears the way to identify the items on the list of wants as *values*, a value being – as the *New Oxford Dictionary of English* (1998) confirms – anything we prize, find useful and regard as important, and to which we feel attracted, as revealed, I would like to add, mostly by how we choose to spend our time and resources, and not simply by what we say. So we might tell people we know well and trust that we value their friendship, or we value peace and quiet, if we are thoughtful types.

This lets me propose that we as humans have a natural way of valuing some things, from water to wealth and wisdom, and rejecting others. I want to use a technical word for this very basic feature of our make-up, by referring to humans as *valorising beings* – beings who are so made that our survival and prospects of flourishing require that we value certain things and avoid others. But our very valorising natures are also a problem for us, because a moment's reflection on ordinary experience shows that we sometimes value things that are harmful to us and to others. Pleasure in excess is the most obvious example, never more so than with alcohol or sex, which, as we all know, can both all too readily degenerate into abuse of others and harm to ourselves. Power is another example, and so is food. Without a fondness for food, we ail and die, but too much fondness can also do us in, though more slowly. In other words, *to live is to value, and to live well is to value wisely and well.*

Support for what I am saying comes from process thought, a school of philosophy that emphasises that whatever enhances the quality of our experiences has value for us. The more comprehensively and intensively it does so, the more the value it has (Whitehead 1933;

Prozesky 1995). Let me link this to my own use of well-being as a governing value. Actions that we find over lengthy periods to have great value, because they enhance our well-being, earn a very high level of approval. We judge them to be right and good, and therefore give them value. Examples that come easily to mind are keeping promises, ensuring that we remain fit, and showing appreciation for friends or colleagues.

The role of feelings

Now comes a most important part of this appeal to our experience to discover what human nature involves: the importance of feelings. Merely listing our wants and aversions is little more than a mental game with concepts such as love, respect, happiness, misery and fear. Instead, it is vital to use our imaginations in order to focus realistically on how we actually experience these things, and once we do so, we see very clearly that our feelings are prominent. To love and be loved is to feel great happiness, and sometimes, great joy. To be afraid is to feel dread, anxiety and a powerful desire to get away from whatever causes the fear. So we need to be very realistic about what it feels like to have the things we want most from life for ourselves and those we care about. So too, with the things that we don't want. We need to picture both the attractions and the aversions as clearly as possible from actual experience and recall how they felt as vividly as possible.

It feels good to know friendship, to be respected, to have enough wealth to enjoy the good things of life, or to have pain relieved. Just as strong are the negative feelings that come with whatever we want to avoid: the desolate feelings that go with rejection or shame, the mental pain of failure, the physical pain of injury and the bitter feelings of anger and resentment that are the experience of the oppressed, not to speak of the despairing anguish of an orphaned and hungry street-child whom nobody wants, or the feelings of emotional pain many of us experience when we think about such suffering in a little child.

By focusing on these feelings, we can see how close the link is between our values and our emotions. The seventeenth-century French philosopher and mathematical genius Blaise Pascal understood this better than most when he wrote in his *Pensées* in 1670 that 'the heart has its reasons of which reason knows nothing' (quoted in Burkill 1971: 347). He understood a basic truth about our human make-up, that we are beings with powerful feelings and that our feelings incline us very strongly to value and pursue some things and to reject others, steering ourselves away from the latter as best we can, without necessarily understanding in our rational minds why we make the choices we do. We are, in short, *sentient* valorising beings, sentience being the capacity to feel pleasure and pain and other emotions and sensations.

The British academic John H. Crook has given us a helpful map of our built-in equipment for action as human beings. We can easily link it to the way conscience works. Crook says that we have four interacting systems:

- a perceptual system (i.e. our senses), which feeds into
- a cognitive system (i.e. our ability to gather and recall *information*);
- a motivational system that *chooses* particular courses of action; and
- a bio-energy system to put our choices into *practice* (Crook 1980: 24ff.).

If we think of our motivational systems as *sentient, valorising systems* – brain-based abilities that allow us to prefer some things to others, then Crook's ideas fit very neatly into what I have been saying about values and feelings. Process thought offers a similarly helpful insight here by reminding us of the way we grade our experiences past, present and anticipated, according to the value we find in them, and that we find value in ways that involve our feelings, as well as our reason.

We can thus think of ourselves as highly mobile focal points of intelligent, value-seeking energy, with significant potential for goodness and a hunger for a quality of fulfilled life that needs the resources of the surrounding world and other people. The person of conscience, the morally thoughtful and effective person, is one who imagines valued outcomes, and then enacts them for the benefit of all concerned, so far as this is reasonably possible.

We can thus also see ourselves as adventurous clusters of energy, organised and self-organising for maximum fulfilment. So, both as individuals and as communities, we become the agents in whom the cosmos seeks expression for its richest potential, its noblest values.

Well-being

My next move, still in the first step of looking at what we want most, is to group the things people say they want most in life into a single category, which I call well-being, and to label the items on the positive list as various aspects of an inborn, natural desire for well-being (Griffin 1986: 40ff.; Prozesky 1984: 102ff.). An effective way of explaining this proposal is to look at happiness, enjoyment and pleasure and to ask ourselves why we want them. The answer that we end up with is that *we just do*. These experiences are satisfying in themselves. Evidently we are made in such a way that they are inherently desirable to us, just as their opposites of pain, suffering, misery and despair are experiences we naturally find unpleasant.

This being agreed – and readers are urged to satisfy themselves about this as well – we can also ask why we want any of the other items on the list, such as health, wealth, or respect? We want to be healthy because we *like* good health. We like what we can do when we are fit and well, and we dislike being unwell. When the question is pressed further, people tell me they like good health because it is part of what it takes to be happy and to enjoy life. So too, with respect. We experience a deep kind of satisfaction when others esteem or admire us, and if asked why we want satisfaction of this kind, the answer again is that *we just do*. The satisfaction we feel is inherently valuable to us, given our make-up. Religious people often say the same about faith. For them, living in tune with what they see as sacred and holy brings a sense of peace, meaning and joy like no other experiences that they find valuable.

So then, what we want from life for ourselves and for those we care about boils down to a few very basic experiences such as happiness, enjoyment and satisfaction. The *New Oxford Dictionary of English* (1998) says that well-being is the word for the 'state of being comfortable, healthy or happy', so it is just the term I need to summarise the set of experiences we all want most from life. As this term is central to my understanding of conscience in practice, we need to look into it in some detail before proceeding further with this journey of self-discovery.

There are views of ethics that focus on happiness, and I have sympathy with them because all of us want to live happy lives. But these views also suffer from a fatal flaw as far as I am concerned. Happiness is a quality of *personal* experience. It is something we feel *individually*. This gives it a subtle bias towards individuals and their emotions, which I find problematic because one of the lessons of history is that more is needed in ethical living than simply individual people feeling happy. After all, drugs can do that for us, while slowly killing us at the same time. The same applies to physical pleasure, and our individual happiness can often come at some cost to others.

In other words, a happiness- or pleasure-based approach to life and to conscience, especially if the emphasis is placed on the individual, runs the risk of subtly undermining the main function of conscience, which is to take us beyond ourselves to a willingness to be concerned also for others – others being understood not only as people, but also as animals, the rest of the natural environment, and also the built environment.

What is required, instead, is what we could call *objective* well-being, namely contexts and societies marked by freedom, protection, justice and peace, in which personal fulfilment and feelings of happiness can be lasting, rich and above all, widespread. The term 'well-being' captures this broader requirement. It has a subjective or personal aspect, which we can speak of as happiness or enjoyment, but is also broad enough to have an objective and more general aspect. This more general aspect refers to the contexts and conditions involving nature, political and economic systems and other people, which are needed in order to make an enriched, creative, caring and responsible personal life possible. Those contexts are also needed in order to support the individual conscience and to deter the greedy. Just why this broader aspect that includes but extends beyond the individual is essential even for lasting personal well-being is something that will be discussed further in the next chapter.

Thus the picture of conscience and well-being that I am painting in this book has to be an *applied* ethic, with things to say about good and bad government, economic systems, education, religion and the like, though it is not the purpose of this book to explore those applications, but rather to make a contribution to the foundations of a global conscience. It is a project that is at once personal, social and environmental, saying that our natural desire for happiness and enjoyment cannot be lastingly satisfied unless it is built on a foundation that will provide the same things for others as well. Conscience must thus be both social and individual.

Here too, the old South Africa is a vivid example. For nearly 350 years, those in power sought the good things of life for themselves at the expense of the great majority of other people. This gave rise to a long and tragic exercise in cruel futility because such selfishness, such lack of concern for others, merely fuelled the undying resentment and resistance of the oppressed and finally their implacable opposition. These feelings may be driven out of sight by the use of violence, but they tick away nonetheless, a time bomb waiting to explode, unless it is defused. Mercifully for South Africa, it is now being defused in our fledgling democracy.

When, then, is well-being present? While it is up to the people of the commonwealth of conscience, the moral democracy, to work together for an agreed vision of human and environmental flourishing, some broad requirements can already be identified. One of them is that true well-being involves the fulfilment and enjoyable functioning of the *whole* person. So there must be health and material satisfaction, but also emotional and social flourishing, and scope for the dimension of our natures that can perhaps be called spiritual, so long as this term is used broadly enough to embrace all people, and not only those with religious faith of the traditional kind.

Another feature of true well-being, much emphasised already, is that it must be as *inclusive* as possible, extending our concern far beyond just our own kind. It is not much of a conscience in our day and age that works only for the good of our own language group, ethnic community, religion or nation. This is why I sometimes call my view of conscience 'a global ethic of *inclusive* well-being'.

This insistence on maximum inclusiveness is particularly important and urgent for the USA at this time, with its apparent fondness for domination and go-it-alone policies in the Middle East after 9/11. There is no way a global culture of genuine, lasting well-being can be fostered by such policies because they undermine the crucial moral values of human equality, justice, respect for other nations and especially, a willingness to restrain national power in order to foster a shared quest for the global good.

There are of course other, much less mighty nations with a similar taste for military domination. At their own levels, they too do great harm to the quest for an inclusive ethic, but only the USA has the power to dominate the entire planet militarily. This is why the movement for a practical global ethic must keep emphasising the highly problematic position of that country in the movement at this time. However, this emphasis on the USA in no way means turning a blind eye to other less military powers that do not have the global reach of that country.

I return now to the requirements for the well-being that we all by nature want so badly. Such well-being will be genuinely and lastingly present for individuals and nations when as many as possible – ideally all those concerned – have the material benefits of good nourishment, safety, health, strength, fitness and access to healing needed for enjoyable physical functioning; when they have skills, information, sources of guidance, opportunities for satisfying work and for growth; when they have freedom, harmonious social relationships and friendships; when they have a sense of beauty and deep meaning whether religious or secular; and when they have an awareness of personal worth and dignity reinforced by the respect of others. When these conditions are present, they bring maximum absence of suffering on one hand, and on the other, the greatest fulfilment and happiness in a safe, clean, beautiful and durable environment.

Maximising well-being
Having discussed in some detail the meaning of well-being, we can now return to the exploration of ordinary human experience as a way of gaining insight into our human nature. At this stage of the process in my workshops and other presentations, I draw people's attention to the fact that we don't only want well-being in its various facets. Most of us want *more* of it. For example, few of us are content with sufficient wealth just to be comfortable. Most of us would like to do better than that in order to enjoy things we would otherwise only dream about, and to know the enjoyment of sharing them with others. For example, I have visited many wonderful parts of the world, but still find myself longing to see them again and to explore others, such South Africa's Drakensberg Mountains, the Australian outback, the Nile River, the Pacific North-West of the USA, the Moscow-St Petersburg waterway, or the Trans-Siberian railway.

We all hear about or imagine new opportunities, new fulfilments, and new pleasures. We want to experience them and then we set about trying to achieve them. So we come to see ourselves not only as beings in pursuit of fulfilment and happiness and out to avoid suffering, but as beings with a drive to *maximise* well-being, to experience ever more of it, and especially to avoid future hardship and suffering. Some of us, to be sure, may feel content with what we have and don't actively pursue greater material prosperity, but contentment is itself a form of subjective well-being, and those who feel it don't want to lose or lessen it.

We can see this human drive to maximise well-being vividly if we reflect for a moment on the story of our human presence on this planet in comparison with the other intelligent primate species, such as chimpanzees and gorillas, and in fact with any other species. Zoology tells us that we humans are biologically very close indeed to those other primates, and I have no problem with this finding. The tendency to set ourselves radically apart from other members of the animal kingdom has exacted a terrible price. It fosters in us the deadly notion that those other beings exist for our benefit and that we have absolute power of life and death over them, which has led to a terrible history of cruelty to animals and species extinctions.

But to face up to this evil is not to deny that there are differences, only that they appear not to be differences of kind, but rather of quantity. Our brains are much bigger; our hands are much more deft; our upright gait on two legs far more liberating for our eyes (by giving them a higher viewpoint), and also more liberating for our arms and hands. It frees them for creative work in ways not open to any other creatures on this planet. These are not trivial differences. Even greater is the difference brought about by our human evolution of language-based cultures.

As a result, our human story since the earliest of our forebears is one of radically greater change than those of any other intelligent species. They remain locked into their native habitats: the gorillas in their misty, verdant mountains, the chimpanzees and bonobos, for all their intelligence, in their lowland forests, the large-brained dolphins in their oceans. We, on the other hand, have reinvented our habitats again and again, moving from woodland to savannah, from scavenging to hunting, from there to the life of nomadic pastoralists with our goats, sheep and cattle, from there to riverbank farming and the first towns, and onward to the New Yorks, Sydneys, Tokyos and Sowetos of today. Placed back where we began, we would very soon perish, even those of us who live in and know the Africa where our human story began.

Why has all of this happened if not because of a relentless hunger for better times, for greater comfort and less vulnerability? And why would our species have experienced these desires again and again, forever imagining better worlds (just as I am, in writing this book), if not because of a drive to *maximise* the satisfactions that we, by our very nature, value so supremely?

Maximise can mean a greater quantity of something, such as money, but it can also mean a better quality of enjoyable experience, such as a deepening friendship or greater career fulfilment. It is very important that we see this in our own experience, recognising that a very deeply valuable kind of satisfaction can happen even when there is real pain. Mothers giving birth know this best, but all of us will recall times when we sacrificed something, or endured some kind of loss for the sake of a loved one, and felt deeply good about it. For conscience, this is a priceless reality because it shows that caring for others and making sacrifices for them does not have to mean real loss for ourselves. And even if it does mean real loss, if it is for the greater good, then many people find it worthwhile, such as in the case of the 'waste' of 27 years of Nelson Mandela's life in prison, or Gandhi's hunger strikes. It shows that we are equipped for experiencing depths of fulfilment and even joy that go far beyond mere physical pleasure.

We have here part of the reason why self-sacrifice – which seems on the surface to decrease well-being for the one who makes the sacrifice, rather than increasing it – takes place. There are of course powerful religious reasons for self-sacrifice in all the spiritual traditions. Christians might think of the poverty and sufferings of Christ, or of Saint Francis of Assisi. Muslims may think of the way Muhammed suffered and had to flee his native city of Mecca. The Buddha gave up a life of comfort to search for enlightenment. People like these and their followers respond to a sense of transcendence, which for them far outweighs the appeal of life's ordinary attractions and pleasures. The kind of fully inclusive, global conscience I am trying to promote respects and supports those reasons, but also argues that we must find independent grounds for a commitment to live in ways that can involve self-sacrifice for others, while still maximising the well-being we all want.

Here are those grounds. Remember first that the whole point of living by the power of conscience is to steer us towards active concern for the good of others, and away from selfishness. This means giving of our time, resources, energy, and at times, our comfort to others. In rare cases, it means giving up our freedom and even our lives. The USA experienced this very powerfully during the civil rights campaign in the 1960s, and a decade later, during resistance to the war in Vietnam. In South Africa, we learnt the same lesson in the long struggle to defeat apartheid. Sometimes conscience calls for great sacrifices, for there are evils that do not go quietly or easily.

But in what way does this promote well-being? To answer this question, we must again remember that well-being is a much richer reality than personal pleasure, which can very clearly be lessened by self-sacrifice. Many of us know from experience that it is possible to suffer while still feeling a deep sense of satisfaction when we make a significant sacrifice for others.

Remember also that well-being has both a personal or subjective side, and a wider, objective side made up of others and the environment. As I will show in Chapter Three, our own personal well-being depends very much on a favourable context. We help to create, strengthen and maintain this favourable context of objective well-being when we give of ourselves for the good of others. We damage it for ourselves and others when we live selfishly.

Add to this the fact that human nature gives us an ability to feel love, sympathy and compassion for others and we have enough grounds for believing that a life governed by conscience and the sacrifices it involves is not only good for others, but also good for us, and especially for the future selves we will be. It is essential to see that as an active commitment to the common good, conscience has a definite future dimension. It is not only about well-being now, but also about well-being in the years, decades, generations and centuries ahead, about the kind of context we, our children and grandchildren will experience in the times to come, not to mention our descendants in the more distant future. Any thoughtful person can therefore see the importance of lifestyles that by self-giving add real value to the wider world of others, now and in the years ahead.

At this stage of the exploration of human nature with my audiences, the more thoughtful members often voice a crucial further insight, also based on experience. We don't only value greater well-being or more enjoyment; *we also want it to last.* Maximum well-being must logically also mean long-lasting, sustainable well-being, for how much real value is there in merely temporary, short-term flourishing and happiness? Not a lot.

Confirmation from brain science

Such, then, is what ordinary human experience reveals about our hunger for enjoyment and satisfaction, which I am presenting as something inborn and thus as a fact of human nature that all people share, irrespective of cultural factors. Could I be deluded here, since experience is prone to error and confusion, seen clearly in the long-held but wrong belief, based on visual experience, that the sun circles the earth, and since there are many people (some Marxists, for example) who would deny that there is such a thing as human nature? To set aside this possibility, I turn now to science for support. There is plenty of it in the form of brain science. Resting on the most reliable knowledge-finding method available to us on matters like this, scientific backing is of course especially powerful. So it matters a great deal that what we learn by reflecting on our own experience, along with that of others, has scientific support. Here is what I have found by consulting experts and texts in human neurobiology. As these are technical issues, I will quote from a more general book by James B. Ashbrook and Carol Rausch Albright called *The Humanizing Brain* (1997).

What is physically most distinctive about the human animal is a huge brain, especially a greatly enlarged cortex. The other parts of the brain are not so distinctive, since we share them with other species. Thus we have brain stems that programme and activate our bodies for self-preservation, readying the body for fight, flight or freeze responses. Ashbrook and Albright refer to this structure as the primal or reptilian brain because it is also present in reptiles, which makes it a very old and well-tried organ, going back in evolutionary time to long before mammals and humans emerged. A being equipped with such a brain structure will experience a very strong impulse to protect, preserve and reproduce itself, especially if these instincts are connected with powerful feelings of pleasure.

For our sentience, our ability to feel pleasure and pain, we must look to another ancient endowment, the limbic lobes positioned above the brain stem. Here we move into what is sometimes called the old mammalian brain, where we find the reticular structures that equip us to feel emotion, which, as Ashbrook and Albright say, 'is motivator and mobilizer' (1997: 73) – precisely what I have been arguing about the role of feelings. The same limbic system is also where memory is located. A moment's reflection will show how this fits into my view of human nature and our hunger for fulfilment. Memory allows us to retain the value of good and bad experiences by keeping alive for us the link between what we felt and what we were in touch with when we felt it, the experience of fire being perhaps the most obviously powerful example. This leads us to expect the same connection in future, so giving us potent incentives to seek out and retain what memory allows us to link with pleasure and happiness, and to avoid what we have learnt to link with pain or suffering. Clearly, good, enjoyable experiences drive us strongly towards favoured external realities linked with them in our memories, which is exactly what I mean by a drive to maximise well-being.

All this we apparently share with many other members of the animal kingdom, unlike our much-enlarged cortex. The latter gives us the abilities we often see as most distinctive about human beings: the powers of language, self-consciousness, freedom in its most basic form (which is the ability to think of different ways of acting, choose between them and then enact the one we choose), and above all, conscience, abilities we will explore later in this chapter. But we must not lose sight of the crucial fact that these enhanced abilities are linked in the brain with those reptilian and mammalian minds of ours, and therefore with powerful impulses to preserve ourselves and those who depend on us, and with feelings of pleasure and pain.

All in all, then, there are good scientific grounds from neurobiology for seeing the drive for well-being as part and parcel of human nature because it involves brain structures we do not choose and cannot change. They are not the fruits of human culture, but its biological basis.

Confirmation from the history of conscience

Our self-understanding as sentient, valorising beings with a drive to maximise well-being is supported further by the evidence of the history of our sense of right and wrong. By this I do not mean the history of (particularly Western) moral philosophy. I am referring to the history of the world's most influential value systems, the most widespread, long lasting and influential of them being faith-based. I have in mind especially those that began to emerge from around 500 BCE in western, southern and eastern Asia, and those that grew from them in one way or another, the so-called world religions and value-systems: Judaism, Christianity, Islam, Upanishadic Hinduism, Jainism and Buddhism in India, Taoism and Confucianism in China, and even Marxism. This is a subject I explored at great length in an earlier book called *Religion and Ultimate Well-Being*, where the details can be found (Prozesky 1984: 184ff.). For present purposes, a brief summary will be enough to make the essential point, namely that the core values of these and many other belief-systems confirm independently what human nature shows about us.

Recall now the huge amount of human energy, passion and commitment that these great movements have summoned from people, including, in some devotees, a willingness to die for what they hold sacred. What else can this mean, other than a deep conviction that in these belief- and value-systems, devotees sense something of surpassing value and importance, a pearl of great worth, for which everything else is sold, the jewel in the lotus, the abiding amidst the fleeting? What else does it mean, other than that in these people, numbering by far the most who have ever lived, there is a concern for the greatest value, for maximum worth, a concern that appears in different forms in every known culture? If this does not reveal something more deeply implanted in us than our culture-based identities of language and custom, nothing ever will. It reveals in our species a profound and abiding concern for that which we sense has greatest value for us.

There is more to be drawn from this evidence. Consider next that from these great belief- and value-systems, the adherents receive what they see as a supremely important message: that by living the required life and holding the required beliefs, directed to that which is supremely important and valuable – understood variously as God, nirvana or Brahman, and so on – there awaits them the supreme blessing of eternal and perfect bliss. It is hard to think of a greater well-being than that. Small wonder that the words used by believers for this most ultimate of destinations – heaven, paradise, *shalom*, the dream-time and the like – have become standard ways of expressing that which is most to be desired and enjoyed, even in secular life.

Thus we find that at a deep and often unnoticed level, the most powerful belief- and value-systems of history, the latest brain science and our own repeated human experience, irrespective of major cultural differences, hold before us a mirror in which we can see with great clarity that we are indeed at heart sentient, valorising beings with a drive to maximise well-being, a drive that is ours by nature, resting as it does on brain structures with which we are born.

What we are not born with, however, is the knowledge of what to value most and why, only with the brain structures to find out, and to decide whether to base our lives on it. Before we explore this side of our make-up, our ability to learn and grow towards and choose between greater goodness or greater evil, we need to discover three other basic features of our make-up, which are hard-wired into our existence: our interconnectedness with others, our creativity and our ethical nature, which means our ability to decide whether conscience will govern our actions or selfishness, greed and dishonesty. We will explore these by taking the next three steps on our journey of self-discovery.

EXPERIENCING OUR RELATIONAL SELVES

Life is a song sung by choirs, not soloists. This is because life is through and through relational, a word referring to the way things are so inextricably linked to others that they cannot function without them. At a superficial level, this is obvious. We are here because of our parents, and we live in families or other groups. We need particular places as homes. We need the resources of the natural environment. The tides of the world's oceans happen because of the moon's gravitational pull, the seasons because of the tilting of the earth's axis. All this is perfectly clear. What is less well known is the deeper reality of our relational natures. To grasp this, we need once more to journey into and question our ordinary human experience. This too is something that I have done often with various audiences, just as I am now putting it to the readers of this book.

I ask my audiences what they think a person is. Who are we really? What are we really? The usual variety of answers comes in: we are large-brained apes, children of God, freaks of evolution, reincarnated mosquitoes, or temporary swarms of atoms – interesting answers all of them, but very much disputed. What, then, in Western societies anyway, would most people agree that we are? I answer the question myself, quoting a splendid phrase I once heard at a presentation by Professor Felicity Edwards, then at Rhodes University in South Africa: we are skin-enclosed egos. Where this might be embarrassing for some people from cultures where the thought of nakedness is a taboo, I say that maybe we are skin-enclosed egos draped in whatever clothes we happen to be wearing.

Put a bit differently, this is the view that the real me, the real you, begin somewhere inside us, like the brain or mind, and end at the skin and its mantle of clothing, which, after all, reveals so much about who we are. This is our personal boundary where we end, moving outwards from our core. It is where we seem to begin when moving inward from whatever is outside us. This skin-enclosed ego becomes a legal being at birth (or at conception, according to some) and ends at bodily death; it is given a starting date and a name and other exclusive markers, such as a social security or identity number.

All of this is true enough and legally very important. Something like this seems to anchor the passion for individual worth that is so strong in most Western societies, and perhaps elsewhere too. But if this is all we think we are, then ours is a very meagre and flimsy sense of personal existence, leaving out much that is exceedingly important about us, such as the drive for the greatest well-being that we have already explored and the deep-level, invisible relationality that we will now consider.

The truth is that as well as being individuals with bodies and therefore having our own personal outer, physical boundaries, we are also rich in-dwellings of the many others whose influence has flowed past our bodily perimeters and into our deeper selves. We are interconnected. Others live on in us, and we live on in them.

To illustrate this point, I ask my audiences to join me in a short thought-experiment. I ask them to heed very carefully what happens when I speak to them and they hear me and understand what I am saying. Being inclined to an occasional theatrical move, I then pause for a moment to let the minds in front of me ready themselves into the necessary expectation and alertness. Then I say something slowly and firmly, like 'We are not just skin-enclosed, clothes-wearing egos; we are mosaics, ensembles, choirs . . .'

Then I pause again, after which I comment on what has just happened to them as follows. (It is also happening right now to anybody reading these words.) I mention the obvious things first: that from my brain and the history of personal experience stored in it, signals have travelled to my lips and from them, as sound waves, across the air to their ears, and then onward as wondrous signals to their brains, where something even more amazing happens to anybody who understands the message. There it fuses with whatever is already lodged in their minds. There it is processed into something *meaningful* to them and becomes part of their beings, and there it will be for the rest of their existence. Mostly the words they hear and all the other signals they receive will sink quite soon into the subconscious part of their brains, seemingly lost, but in fact still there and able to be reawakened and to influence them.

The same, I add, has been happening to me during this exercise, for as I uttered whatever I said, I was watching my audience closely, my eye caught by a sudden movement, or widening of somebody's eyes, or by a yawn, or an expression of dawning insight of the kind so dear to educators such as myself. These messages embed themselves forever in my mind, becoming part of my being.

And this is what is happening to us all the time, so that we both receive and give influences to all who experience us, making individuals into choirs (with ourselves as conductors, perhaps) rather than only individual soloists. The process philosopher, Alfred North Whitehead had a memorable phrase for this reality in his great but difficult book *Process and Reality*, originally published in 1929, writing that in this reality, 'the many become one and are increased by one' (Whitehead 1978: 21).

To return to the central word in this section – relational – we can now appreciate the deeper reality of our *relational* natures, the reality that our innermost beings are both givers and receivers of influence involving all that we encounter. Even more important, we can also see that this process can be both beneficial and harmful, not only when we speak or act intentionally, but also from the kind of presence we are as we walk, or stand, or sit. Do we send a message that by its beauty and goodness is pleasing and enriching, or one that disturbs and menaces? Does our presence add value and appeal to the world we influence, or reduce value and inject ugliness? Does that ambient world add value for us or reduce it? How are we to find fulfilment under the sometimes-huge weight of the surrounding world and its impact on us? These are the key questions for sentient, valorising and relational beings like you and me, who have come to understand that the harm we do to others harms us too by damaging the social and natural environments on which we all depend, even though that harm can bring us short-term, selfish pleasures, just as goodness done to others is also goodness done to ourselves.

Earlier in this chapter I quoted from Ashbrook and Albright in connection with the brain structures that anchor our sentience and the drive for well-being that it triggers and partly directs. Now the question is whether the same brain science also shows that relationality is part of our very natures, and the answer again, is that it does. Very early in their book, Ashbrook and Albright write as follows: 'Knowledge of the brain's development states that relatedness is the primary reality that liberates rather than constricts' (1997: xxvii). They go on to say that our brains are hard-wired to seek out and respond to the human face, adding that the 'face of another human being calls forth who we are. We are created to relate' (1997: 16).

However, relationality is not only a human reality. It is also true of the world around us, indeed of the entire cosmos, as modern science confirms, bringing to light both the fact of an interconnected universe, and also, as a result, the mistaken belief in individual self-sufficiency. Africa's traditional wisdom has always understood the fact of relationality better than the greedy, selfish culture that has captivated so many of us in the rich, developed world. Zulus and some other black Africans call it *ubuntu* – a word meaning that we can only be persons in and through other persons (Shutte 2001: 16ff.; for the kind of culture involved, see also Thorpe 1991: 30ff.). In Zimbabwe's Shona language, the word is *ukama*. But here it has the added meaning that we can only be human in and through other people *and nature* (Murove 1999: 10ff.).

As judged by an outsider like me – albeit an extremely interested one – the sciences that are most obviously relevant here are genetics and ecology, for both of them reportedly give grounds for accepting that life on this planet must be seen as an interconnected whole, with no fundamental dividing lines separating the various species, or their members from one another, or the whole of life from its natural environment. Instead, there is a single, inclusive web of life, inseparably linked to and embedded in the soil, the air and the waters of the earth, sharing a common chemistry and a common physics in a single known cosmos, across which the same laws of science hold good.

The energy that pulses in our lives at this very moment goes back to the Big Bang itself, assuming that it really is the beginning point of the physical universe, like all energy in the universe. And – nearer home now – we humans share the same tree of life as all other living things. While it is perhaps hard for some of us to acknowledge a degree of real kinship with spinach and prickly pears, the kinship is there. Like it or not, life is a togetherness thing, and in that case, it is mere superficiality and ignorance to go on believing, as some of us do, that we humans are simply skin-enclosed egos, or that there can be genuinely such a thing as individual self-sufficiency.

For conscience, the meaning of this fact of relatedness is as follows: *lasting* personal well-being – the only kind any intelligent being would want – is inseparably bound up with general well-being. Once the interrelatedness of all things is understood, and our most persuasive sources of knowledge very much confirm it, then the power of rational thought comes into play, by showing why selfishness cannot in the end deliver what we want most – the richest and most durable of satisfactions. Only considerate and fundamentally truthful living can do this, truthfulness being essential because as individuals and societies, we cannot thrive without sound information, and information must be true in order to be sound. I will return to this crucial point in the next chapter.

From modern science, we can turn again to the world's great belief-systems, for there we find, if we look deeply, further affirmation of the relationality under discussion, a relationality that embraces the whole of reality. This is what it means to believe that there is a single creator of everything in the universe, as Christians, Jews, Muslims and others do. This is also the implication of the great Buddhist doctrine of inter-dependent origination, which holds that everything exists in a network of mutual influence and causation, and of the classical Hindu idea of the identity of Brahman and Atman, of the great cosmic soul – Brahman – and the individual soul, or Atman, in all of us.

Believers will take these teachings as supremely authoritative; for others they serve a lesser but still instructive purpose, namely that for all their surface differences of doctrine, these massively influential and very long-standing belief- and value-systems have taught the very point so tellingly made by modern science, that ours is a relational cosmos, a single, seamless totality where things affect other things in a ceaseless play of mutual influences.

Seen from a different angle, which will be explained in detail later in the fourth section of this chapter, morality arises from the inter-connected diversity of our existence precisely because there is so much variety in our world. It is because of this variety and difference that options are available to us, which give rise to choices, and choices are part and parcel of the very meaning of conscience, ethics and morality. Embedded in a world of difference where choices are possible, we humans are made in such a way that we constantly seek the greatest well-being. We can do so selfishly, or we can do so considerately. The choice is ours.

From this fact of universal relatedness, for fact it is, comes another key point for the great adventure of conscience, a point to which I have already referred. This is the illusion of individual self-sufficiency. I am not for a moment opposing a belief in the great value of individual life, let alone its reality, as will be made very clear in the next section of this chapter. What is being rejected as false and dangerous is the notion of individual self-sufficiency, that we can go it alone, and with it, the false and harmful idea that community and society are trivial matters before the so-called sovereignty of the individual.

In a cosmos that is thoroughly interrelated, and in a human world that is also undeniably interrelated, there can clearly be no such thing as an individual who can exist as a self-contained ego. The truth is that we are neither individually sovereign, nor individually subject, but both, as the next section will explain. We need the world and the world, or at least our corner of it, needs us. It creates us and we create it. Perhaps this creativity is what Judaism and Christianity mean with their belief that humans are made in the image of their creator, receiving but also giving transforming influences throughout their lives – a good point from which to proceed to the next step in our exploration.

DISCOVERING OUR CREATIVITY

Earlier in this chapter when we were discussing the desire to maximise well-being, I drew attention to the astonishingly radical way in which our species has invented and reinvented itself again and again, from a creature barely beyond knuckle-walking to one who has set foot on the moon, and is preparing to do so on Mars. In doing so, I was of course already touching on the marvellous creative power that we possess. This much is apparent to anybody who knows anything about our story as a species.

What often happens is that creativity – the ability to bring about something genuinely new – is often seen, especially in the arts, as the preserve of very gifted people, such as Mozart or Shakespeare. This is a mistake. Creativity is a reality in everybody, though obviously not to the same extent, or in the same spheres. But in our own ways, all of us, every day of our lives, even every minute, live creatively. As much as our drive for the greatest well-being and our relationality, the power to produce something genuinely new is part of our very natures.

Recall that this book calls for a post-obedience ethic, which requires all of us to take responsibility for strengthening the moral fabric of our own lives, our societies and the world as a whole. Clearly, this is a task calling for the ability to *find* ways of handling whatever problems we encounter. Just as clearly, it calls for creative effort. The whole project would fail if people did not have this ability. If we are really just followers and never real leaders, never really the captains of the ships that are our own lives, it is asking far too much to urge people everywhere to become co-creators of a better future. So it is essential that we have direct awareness of our own creativity, especially in the depths of our natures as conscious, thinking beings.

To bring the point home to my audiences, I therefore illustrate our innate creativity as follows, in a way that everybody can experience for himself or herself. I remind my audiences of our previous thought experiment where they attended carefully to something I said, noticing how my message became part of their very beings, with their own messages, in the form of body language, doing the same for me. Now I take this demonstration a step further, this time drawing a shape like the one here on the flip-chart or chalkboard, and ask them what they see, just as I now invite readers to think about what they see.

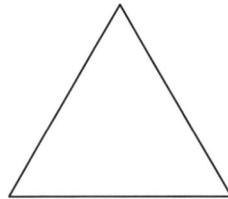

Invariably the answer is that they see a triangle, but now and then, somebody says that he or she sees a pyramid. This is just what I want to hear because it lets me point out that to see a triangle or a pyramid, or anything else, involves far more than just seeing. Strictly speaking, all they *see* is three straight lines drawn in white or yellow chalk (or whatever) meeting at three points. To 'see' a triangle or a pyramid, their brains must already have some geometry, or knowledge of Egypt, along with their personal educational backgrounds, which they then *actively* use in order to identify the object on the board as a triangle or pyramid. I point out that any one of them could have come up with an entirely different interpretation – for interpretation is really what is happening, not only seeing – 'seeing' the shape as an alien spacecraft, or a letter in extraterrestrial writing, and so on.

What this confirms is firstly that our brains are *active* learning systems, fusing incoming signals with what they already know, or can imagine into a new experience. This involves creativity, not passivity, a reality that is not changed by the fact that people with the same kinds of prior experience will tend to come up with the same kind of interpretation of the incoming signal (Hanson 1969: 61ff.).

The second lesson is that each of us could, if we wished, have come up with different interpretations – especially for a very rich signal. Then creativity takes on a more individualistic form, involving originality. School education, even in democratic countries can, alas, dampen this inborn ability by stressing uniformity and by not doing enough to stimulate the learners' powers of imagination, but they are there, none-theless, however sluggish in some of us.

At the heart of our beings, we are in truth also creative beings, whose hunger for greater enjoyment and fulfilment goes hand in hand with the ability to imagine and then create new ways of meeting this hunger. An ethic that aims at maximum, inclusive well-being is by its very nature an ethic that wants the greatest fulfilment of potential for everybody. This must include, indeed emphasise, the flowering of creativity, not least in our sense of right and wrong, and how we use its power. In other words, conscience is itself a work of art, waiting for us to make it more beautiful. Goodness, real, lasting, widespread goodness can thus be the great and lovely gift we shape for others and ourselves.

This view of conscience is not in the least in conflict with a religious view, which sees a transcendent spirit as the ultimate, creative source of all that is truly valuable and worth having. What it does rule out, as untrue to the facts of experience and as ethically unworthy, is the belief that in the realm of conscience, we are passive beings, mere consumers of values produced and packaged for us somewhere on high, mere foot-soldiers under orders on the battlefield against evil. Instead, its message for religious believers is that the creator they worship and serve is not some 'Celestial Sultan' who governs by absolute decree, but one who, in supreme generosity, brings into being a universe in which the wondrous process of creating generosity, beauty and truth can truly be ours.

EXPERIENCING OURSELVES AS FREE AND ETHICAL BEINGS

We can now think of humanity as a flowering of the world's potential, of cosmic possibility that sometimes goes terribly wrong, but often also wonderfully right because of our freedom to choose. Freedom is the ability to think of different ways of acting, selecting a preferred option, and then acting on it. It is important to notice that every time we do this, we change ourselves. We become, however slightly, what we choose, constantly recreating ourselves.

The prominence of genetics in today's biology may raise doubts about this belief in real human freedom because it looks as if there is a basis in our genes, rather than in our choices, for much of what we are (Hamer 1994: 1ff.). I have no basic problem with that sort of perception. Indeed, my own acceptance of the concept of human nature means that there is much about us that is inborn and is thus in some way presumably caused by genetic factors. What I do reject is the doctrine known as genetic determinism, the view that our genes control the whole of our beings. The evidence of cultural and personal diversity and of our own experience of making choices that go against our bodily inclinations, self-sacrifice being a prime example, is far too great for this doctrine to be the whole truth.

The issue is thus *how free* we are of our genetic make-up, of our inborn drives and desires, not whether we are free of them at all. My own experience and that of all others known to me is that we are free enough to find deep value in choosing to give of ourselves and our possessions to others and in brave episodes of honesty, when sheer self-interest would incline us to put our own interests first. This is quite enough to establish that there is nothing illusory or unreal about human freedom.

Selfhood, truly human selfhood, is thus both the gift and the burden of our creative freedom in a relational world, limited though our liberty is by that world. Therein lies massive potential for self- and world-enhancement, and it is built into us thanks to our brains, with their creative abilities, the ability to understand different options, to grasp their value, and to choose which to adopt.

There is a therefore a further truth to be drawn from the thought experiment of the triangle that we explored earlier in this chapter. Often we think of freedom as freedom of movement, speech, association and the like, or freedom from captivity and control, and these are obviously important notions of freedom. But we need to see more deeply into ourselves, into the core of our beings as thinking, intelligent agents. Reflecting on how we came to 'see' the shape on the chalkboard, or on the page as we did, all of us can at once see our inner freedom of mind at work.

Nobody and nothing *forced* us to see triangles, pyramids, or alien spacecrafts, though background influences do guide the way we interpret raw experience. Our minds did this entirely for themselves. We can be indoctrinated to believe that we are stupid or passive and built for obedience, which can greatly inhibit this inner freedom. But it is never lost, and once we recognise and develop it, it can become a marvellous part of what it means to be most richly human. It can become the power to control how we will think about whatever happens to us, and how we will define ourselves, refusing to let others tell us what we are. It becomes the basis of a self-directed life of goodwill and generosity, a life capable of freely chosen good or evil, thereby opening the doorway to the discovery of ourselves as ethical beings.

It may even open the way to an entirely new and richer sense of what it can mean to be spiritual beings, who freely interact and fuse with whatever we find to be the most valuable and sacred of all realities, as we will see in Chapter Four. We have already discussed that true selfhood is both the gift and the burden of our freedom to make our own decisions. Now we also see that conscience, our moral sense, and our capacity for being held responsible for what we do, is also the gift of that freedom. Why else would we condemn people who create computer viruses, but not the viruses themselves? Because the people who create the viruses choose to do so, and know exactly what they are doing, so we hold them responsible, and not the viruses themselves.

We saw earlier in this chapter that we have an inborn drive to maximise well-being, but not an inborn knowledge of what will satisfy that drive. We have to learn what to value, and also what to value most. A brain that is equipped for new learning – for creativity – is a brain that can take up this challenge in a process of educational and ethical adventure.

As a species, we started in very great ignorance compared to the levels of knowledge in humans of today. When the early environment changed and we had to leave the forests for the grasslands, this ignorance meant great vulnerability, for who could know what would prosper out there? Trial and error became the only way forward, then and ever since. Who knows today what genetic modification will bring and whether we should see it as valuable or not? There is no way of knowing in advance, so all we are left with is to venture as wisely as we can into every new and unknown situation, learning from a harvest of plenty and the happiness it brings that we have found something to value, and from a harvest of failure and suffering to turn back and go somewhere else.

By nature, we prize pleasure and happiness very greatly, but we must also understand that knowing how to find them has a price that must sometimes be paid with pain and failure. Those who bore the brunt of the struggle to defeat racism in the USA and apartheid in South Africa know this truth only too well.

All of this, now amounting to some 200 000 years of experience, according to scientific experts, has been possible because we are equipped for the discovery of what is important, what brings benefit and what does not, and equipped also with the freedom to choose what to emphasise, and what to avoid, or even forbid, such as incest (Tobias 1981: 62ff.). When we understand that we have these options and must choose how to live, we achieve moral status; we become ethically accountable beings, meaning that we can be held responsible for what we do. And when we choose to show active concern for others, to live in this way, and not only for ourselves, we become morally good people – people of conscience.

Never will I forget the feelings that I experienced on that winter's day that I described in Chapter One, when two dark-skinned people came to my rescue - me a white South African - out of the sheer goodness of their hearts, even breaking the law to help me. A quarter of a century later, the power and beauty of their deed still moves and inspires me and always will, more so now than then, when its impact had yet to dawn on me fully.

What those two individuals did was deeply and richly valuable, involving great compassion and kindness, an ability to rise above resentment at the type of person who belonged to the oppressive race, involving also courage and a complete freedom from any desire for material reward. What I felt because of them, and still feel, is a sense of being elevated, being deeply enriched, being helped into a whole new world with a quality of well-being for which I can find no adequate words, except perhaps to think of that morning's event as my most powerful experience of very deep value.

We can all find from our own experience that we are indeed beings equipped for the utterly fundamental, life-directing options of selfishness or inclusive concern, and for choosing what we will embrace. What should we value more: our own personal interests, or the interests of others, as well as our own, and why? How can we tell? Simply by relying on some external authority, or trusting the moral wisdom of the past? I have already emphasised that this book is about a post-obedience conscience, which means showing that there is a better alternative to depending on a perceived moral authority in order to answer these questions. Chapter Three gives my way of answering them, once again drawing on the lessons of experience.

My case for conscience now moves to questions that are absolutely critical in today's world, with its massive emphasis on excessive consumption as the way to the greatest well-being: What is so bad about greed? What is so bad about selfishness? Why care about others? The next chapter sets out my answers.

three

Why Selfishness Self-Destructs

Join me now at one of the world's most beguiling university campuses, the University of California at Santa Cruz. Set amid redwood trees on a hilltop above a great, grassy, sloping meadow between Monterey Bay and the Santa Cruz mountains, its winding roads and attractive colleges are about as far from the soulless concrete campuses of many other universities as you can imagine. It was here, during a sabbatical, that I was invited to attend a session addressed by the then president of the USA's National Endowment for the Humanities (the body that makes federal grants for research in that sector of academic work), Lynn Cheney, wife of the present US Vice-President, Dick Cheney. When it came to question time, one of the graduate students asked her a question expressing the individualistic, self-centred values that challenge conscience to the core: 'Why is it in my rational self-interest to do humanities research?'

Ms Cheney's answer, as I recall, was true to everything that I as an applied ethics professor and former Dean of Humanities have come to cherish in a long academic career. She replied that the questioner was missing the whole point of the humanities, which is that engagement with the spirit and achievements of human beings is its own main reward. She added that it betrays the humanities to sell them as if they were passports to a financially profitable, self-serving life. This may, for some, be an outcome of studying the humanities, but it is not its central justification.

I was deeply impressed by this reply. My own long immersion in the humanities has made me keenly aware that what they offer is something richly valuable, both in and of themselves, and for the wider world: humane wisdom, discovered by opening our minds and spirits to the fruits of human endeavours, past and present, to the nobility and the savagery, the beauty and the ugliness. Nonetheless, I also felt that the young man who asked that question had done us a real favour. He had asked *why*. He had asked why he should consider spending time, effort and money on something that did not further his own personal interests. He could just as well have asked me why I think conscience is such a big deal, why anybody with brains should prefer generosity to greed. He was expressing something that is also part of what makes us the species we are – *Homo sapiens* – the supremely intelligent, thinking animal: our passion for reasons.

During my student days, a friend of mine at Rhodes University in South Africa, and later at Oxford, Tim Couzens, now an award-winning author, published a memorable, two-line poem in a student magazine. With his permission, I quote it here from memory:

'Father, Why?' the child cried.
In that word he lived and died.

One of the marks of human intelligence is the desire for reasons in that child's cry. In the view of conscience taken in this book, asking *why* we should live ethically – why we should do what is good and right – means wanting reasons for being actively concerned for the well-being of others and for being truthful. Why indeed? Why not rather live only for ourselves, cheating and telling lies whenever we think we will gain something by doing so? Perhaps the most revealing symptom of ill health in our human condition today is the lack of a convincing answer to these questions, an answer that works for everybody irrespective of culture, creed, colour, or beliefs.

The purpose of this chapter is to set out, in detail, the following answer to this question: living on the basis of a robust conscience is the *only* way for humanity to achieve what we all want most, and what is in our best interests, namely *maximum, sustainable well-being,* given our make-up as human beings, our ability to choose and the way the world works at a deep level. It is an answer that is supported by personal experience available to anybody on careful reflection, by science, by the wisdom of all the great ethical cultures, and by some logical thinking.

To give my reasons for living caringly rather than selfishly, this chapter develops a case that is again open to anybody and everybody on an equal footing, so meeting the crucial test of any really *ethical* proposal, the test of maximum inclusiveness, respect and fairness. But before we embark on this discussion, we must note both the importance and the insufficiency of religious and Western philosophical grounds for rejecting selfishness, and opting for considerate, ethical living, in an inclusive, global project to transform conscience into a world-enhancing power.

THE VALUE AND LIMITS OF RELIGIOUS MOTIVATIONS

There are plenty of religious reasons for a life marked by concern for the welfare of others, rather than simply being focused on our own well-being. Many Roman Catholics who judge the use of the contraceptive pill to be wrong do so because they take many of their bearings about right and wrong from the authority of the church through the decisions of the popes who have forbidden it. Protestant Christians, with a concern for the poor, base their values on the Bible as they understand it, or on the example of Christ. Muslims follow the teachings of the Qur'an, the example of Muhammed and Islamic tradition. African traditionalists heed the wishes of their ancestors, and follow traditional customs. And so we might go on. For members of these faiths, such motivations are often enough, and much good has come into the world from them, especially in connection with compassion.

Together the world's religions reportedly embrace in excess of 80% of the global population, so their collective influence is quite considerable, even if some members are nominal, rather than committed followers. By any fair reckoning, the power of conscience in the lives of Moses, Jesus Christ, Buddha, Muhammed and other leading religious figures, and their influence on human behaviour is both immense and highly admirable, to say the least; one does not have to be religious to recognise this.

But there are also serious problems. For example, traditional kinds of religious motivation strike me as often underplaying reason because many believers rely more on faith, which is often implanted before they are able to think for themselves, or to consider critically the evidence for and against their beliefs. Nor is much effort given to making evidence available. More seriously for an approach to conscience that includes people of all cultures, religious motivations for rejecting selfishness in favour of ethical living work only within particular faith communities. So they are not inclusive and in their present shape and form cannot be, at least for the foreseeable future. This is because no religion (or secular belief-system, for that matter) shows any sign of winning general human acceptance. It is true that religions such as Buddhism, Judaism, Christianity and Islam claim that their ethical systems apply to all humankind, at least to some extent. However, my point is that in fact, none of these value-systems has won the support of more than a fraction of the world's people, and none shows any sign of doing so. Hindus might be led by the Gita or the Veda, but they do not turn to the Qur'an or the Bible for moral direction, and so on. The net result is a set of different and mostly contradictory motivations. The Bible and the Qur'an cannot both be the last word about faith and morality, since they give contradictory teachings on some central issues, such as the ethics of polygamy and on charging interest on loans. Then there are their incompatible views about the moral authority of Christ. For Christians, he is the Son of God, the Second Person of the Holy Trinity. Muslims revere him as a true prophet, but no more, and definitely not higher than Muhammed in status.

Even within their own areas of influence, some of the religious reasons for ethical living have lost ground for many people. In Western Europe, Australia and elsewhere, Christianity has lost a large number of followers, especially the so-called mainline churches. And in the USA, where churchgoing and synagogue attendance are far more prevalent than in most other Western countries, faith-based reasons for living ethically are weakened by divisions in both Christianity and Judaism. These divisions set conservatives, for whom the commands of the Gospels or the pope, the Torah or the Talmud, are reason enough to live moral lives, against liberals and radicals who reject the idea of uncritical obedience to external authorities.

There are other complications for anybody who thinks that faith-based moral motivations are all the world needs. Many countries are now home to a whole range of religions, each giving its own motivations for unselfish, truthful living, and in some countries, there are now significant numbers of people who reject all religion.

Clearly then, in a religiously pluralistic and partly secularised world, it cannot be enough to call for ethical living just because the Ten Commandments, the Sermon on the Mount, the Qur'an, the dharma, the Tao, the Confucian Analects, or the will of the ancestral spirits say that we should, not to speak of the 'Humanist Manifesto', no matter how sound their core ethical values.

There are those who argue that there is something immature about the answers offered by the world's religions because they rely so heavily on obedience, especially blind obedience. Is this worthy of thinking, informed and responsible beings in an age of democracy? Does it not, in the end, weaken the cause of conscience by fostering a culture of dependency in ethics at a time when we need moral responsibility? An active concern for the good of others means that we must want and work for the fulfilment of everybody's potential. This means striving for maturity and responsible behaviour, most of all in connection with values. It means growing beyond conscience in dependency mode. One of the main claims of this book is that we must transcend what I call 'the ethics of obedience', understood as an uncritical acceptance of the teachings of an external moral authority, which is very unlike the ethics of deep commitment that I support.

In our day and age, with widespread belief in democratic values and a commitment to human equality, obedience of an uncritical kind is for small children and some would say also for soldiers under orders in the heat of battle, not for mature adults.

With the quest for a united, global conscience as our goal, there are thus insuperable limitations in the motivations given by our traditional religions for why we should shun greed and selfishness and be actively concerned for others, for all the valuable inspirations to moral activism that we see in religious leaders such as Martin Luther King Jr. and Desmond Tutu. Traditional religious faiths are too regional, often too inward looking and fond of elevating obedience above liberation, besides at times being insufficiently self-critical. They divide humanity, sometimes to the point of murderous alienation, as we see dreadfully in the Middle East, in the conflict between Catholics and Protestants in Northern Ireland, or between Hindus and Buddhists in the northern part of Sri Lanka.

Of course, it can be asked whether human-based reasons for ethical living are not just as likely to divide humanity. I do not think so, provided that they rest on foundations that are genuinely and fairly open to all people, and that they are not in conflict with religious beliefs about where to turn for moral inspiration. Basing ethical living on human nature, as I am doing, meets this test. The problem with faith-based reasons for doing good is that they appeal to factors that seem inherently unable to unite us, or be shared equally by all, such as a belief in the unique authority of Christ, rather than the Qur'an, and vice versa.

What these problems mean is that while religious motivations for morality will continue to hold sway in various faith communities, where they can be wonderfully effective in fostering compassion, integrity and other ethical values, they cannot provide the united motivation we need as the basis of a global conscience. Something else is needed, something inclusive, something that we can all share as responsible human equals, without alienating either those who do not have religious beliefs of any kind, or those who are religious believers. This chapter about why selfishness fails does exactly that, by building on the realities of human nature explained in Chapter Two. But before I proceed, I need to explain why Western philosophy cannot do the job either.

PHILOSOPHY: BRILLIANT BUT IMPOTENT

Philosophy as we know it in the English-speaking world makes no calls to faith, and especially not to uncritical obedience to authority or tradition. It bows only before the authority of informed, logical reasoning. In principle, this opens it up to everybody, making it a genuinely inclusive approach to issues of conscience. I shall therefore make much use of the philosopher in all of us, of the power of logical analysis and argument, as an essential part of my case of ethical living – essential but not sufficient, because here too, there are crucial limitations.

While obviously strong on reason, philosophical ethics is, all too often, weak on guidelines for moral action and short of information about moral issues, though the work of Peter Singer (1993) and a few others is a valuable departure from this pattern. The core business of philosophy is to work with concepts and arguments of a highly abstract and theoretical nature, and it does so with great sophistication. This is as true of most moral philosophy as of other branches of the subject, and naturally enough, it has the effect of removing much (but not all) of philosophical ethics from the cut and thrust of the day-to-day world of ethical problems.

If you have any doubts about this, have a careful look at the leading academic journals in moral philosophy from the past decade in any good university library, as I pointed out earlier in this book. Ask questions such as whether the war against Saddam Hussein was morally justified, or whether it is right to permit same-sex marriage and you will wonder what most of the articles in those journals have to do with conscience as an urgent and at times, agonised feature of human existence.

However, this abstraction is not the only problem with Western moral philosophy. Almost without exception, the philosophy books on practical ethics that I have looked at treat Western moral philosophy as if it were the only basis for grappling with ethical issues such as the environment, wealth and poverty, war, the death penalty or sexuality – all of which are global issues affecting far more non-Westerners than Westerners. The assumption seems to be that if you know something about the moral philosophy of Aristotle, Kant, Mill and modern virtue ethics, you have all that you really need in order to address the rights and wrongs of society and the individual (see Blackburn 2001; Frankena 1973; Gensler 1998; Glover 1999; Warnock 1998; Williams 1993).

Those of us who have been influenced by Western philosophy, cannot wipe it from our minds, nor should we, for it has much of real value to offer. But we can see it in the same way as the wisdom and values of other streams of human experience from the East and the South, and we can modify our earlier conditioning in the light of these streams. Basing our ideas about right living only on Western ethics might have been understandable a generation or two ago and earlier, before cultural diversity became as widespread as it is now. Today, it strikes me as intellectually and morally indefensible to hold on to this belief, when people of various cultures and philosophies sit in our classes, browse in our bookshops, and pay our salaries with their taxes. There is so much to be gained from embracing diversity and what other cultures have to offer.

It may be that when we in the West have widened our horizons to include the thinkers of China, India, the Muslim world, Africa and elsewhere, we will all come to agree that Western ethical thought really is the most powerful and advanced, making it a necessary *and sufficient* basis for practical ethics worldwide. What is no longer acceptable, either academically or ethically, is the assumption that the wider world of ethical philosophy beyond the West can simply be ignored. The implicit (and perhaps often unintended) disrespect to other cultures, which is undeniably present in our world, must give way to an active engagement with the moral wisdom of the whole world, and not only the West.

That said, I must add that Western philosophy has been the most valuable of the disciplines I have studied, and I will always recommend and use it. Nonetheless, on its own, it is too abstract, narrowly Western and ineffective to be all we need, as we work towards an effective global conscience.

But even a more comprehensive approach that includes all the world's most influential ethical philosophies, secular and religious, will still not be a strong enough foundation for an ethic of the kind this book proposes and for its motivation, because it will still be under-informed. There are other disciplines with important things to tell us about conscience: history, literature and poetry, psychology, economics, politics, management studies, biology, and even physics, so we need to seek out their contributions as well, widening the study of conscience even more into a richly interdisciplinary process, and getting us out of the mental paddocks that so often limit and weaken our thinking.

So then, conscience as seen by Western philosophy will not be enough to provide an inclusive, effective case against selfishness and for the common good of our planet. It is too theoretical, too Western and too Northern – a metaphor for the privileged world, including its Southern hemisphere members such as Australia, New Zealand, and most of white South Africa. I also think that some of it (like virtually the whole of conservative religion) is also patriarchal. Nearly all the main ethical thinkers in moral philosophy and applied philosophical ethics have been and are male, although important female thinkers of conscience and intellectual power are now mercifully weakening this tradition of male philosophical dominance (see Gilligan 1993; Hursthouse 1995; King 1995; Nussbaum 2000; Ruether 1996).

It is important at this point to note the difference between the way Western philosophers handle issues of conscience and the approach of the three Abrahamic value-systems: Judaism, Christianity and Islam. The former stems from the elites of ancient Greece – for example,

Aristotle, who was the teacher of Alexander the Great. Judaism, Christianity and Islam came to deal with issues of good and evil quite differently: not as issues that mainly challenge our minds, but out of experiences of suffering and social injustice, giving rise to a burning desire to overcome these evils. Passion and action, rather than clarity and precision of thought were their mode of moral engagement, which is one reason for their ability to inspire people in very large numbers to live according to their teachings. To my mind, neither of these approaches – based on reason or on suffering – is enough on its own. However, both are necessary, and both are therefore woven into the fabric of this book.

So then, to inspire a twenty-first-century movement of conscience across the globe, we need more than regional religions and Western philosophy, more than world theology and world philosophy, valuable though they are in their own spheres. We need grounds for decent, caring ways of living that will be *genuinely and maximally inclusive*. The argument in the rest of this chapter is designed to be exactly that – to be more ethical and better informed than is possible when we work inside a single faith tradition, or philosophy, or even within all of them.

WELL-BEING DEPENDS CRUCIALLY ON EXTERNAL FACTORS

Let us pause here and recall briefly what was discussed in the previous chapter. Experience reveals to us our sentient, value-seeking nature and our innate drive to enjoy the greatest well-being. As relational beings in a relational world, we are affected by factors outside of ourselves, like feeling cold when the temperature drops, or anxious when somebody approaches us menacingly, just as we in turn influence others, both favourably and unfavourably. This is what relatedness means.

As *sentient* beings, we feel things that affect us painfully, others that affect us pleasurably, and still others, somewhere in between, or that we meet with indifference. We all recoil from pain; we all want to prolong pleasure, and we don't much mind things that cause us to feel neither. As *creative* beings, we remember these experiences, learn to avoid the things that hurt us, seek out and want to intensify those we enjoyed, and endure the others. The experiences of pleasure, happiness, contentment and whatever we find brings them about become the things that we value, so we deem them good. Their opposites we see as bad, and even evil, when they are especially severe.

Given our drive to find the greatest fulfilment and happiness, and given its power, life becomes for us a process of having to steer ourselves towards whatever we learn to value because of the benefits it brings, and away from what we learn causes us harm and suffering. So we see that a creative, sentient, vulnerable being whose existence is very strongly affected, often adversely, by other such beings and by natural forces, must develop ways to come to terms with these external forces. Such a being must find the best ways to win favour with others and to avoid their hostility, and must zealously foster behaviours that do this. What we call conscience, ethics and morality has its roots in this important project and its beneficial results.

As this summary shows, our drive for maximum well-being is subject to things beyond our control. The world around us affects us variously, now causing harm and pain, now causing benefit and happiness. This is true of the natural environment, with its droughts, cold fronts, frosts and times of bounty, and it is certainly also true of the human environment. Out there, close enough to affect us, there are always other people whose actions can harm us, as well as benefit us, with the added complications that they can do so deliberately and in ways that we may not recognise. A charismatic, attractive teacher, for example, might have a jealous, rival colleague who quietly spreads an untrue but damaging rumour about him, without the former ever knowing who was responsible.

Such is our permanent home on this planet: a surrounding context of people and nature that is ambivalent, capable of aiding, as well as thwarting and even wrecking our hopes of finding greater well-being. This reality is already enough to unsettle us when we think about our powerlessness before some of the forces of nature and the freedom of other people to act as they choose. None of us can control these things or make them do our bidding.

Feeling unsettled and anxious is, of course, not something we enjoy, so it triggers creative powers in us to reduce the anxiety by finding the most secure way to live in the face of this ambivalent surrounding world. What is that way? It starts with a vital choice between two great alternatives that beckon us onward.

THE GREAT CHOICE: GENEROSITY OR GREED?

The step we are about to take is a decisive part of my case for conscience as the passport to greater well-being for our world. Here too, we will need to pay attention to our own experience of life. We will also be using the power of logical reasoning, harnessing the philosopher in all of us. And here too, I recall vividly an experience of my own, directly relevant to my argument at this point, an experience that proved to be richly informative and ethically invaluable.

It took place a few years ago in the truly splendid boardroom of a leading law firm in Sydney, Australia. I was on a visit to the St James Ethics Centre in that city. The Centre kindly arranged for me to give a late-afternoon presentation, the venue being this boardroom high up in a tall building near the magnificent Sydney harbour. Picture it: a longish room, with a large window all along one side, giving a stunning view of the harbour, with the famous bridge at one end of the view and the glorious Opera House at the other. I wondered if I would be able to keep people's attention in competition with such a view!

Anyway, in the audience I noticed a man who nodded enthusiastically at my key points, giving me just the kind of feedback that a speaker before an entirely unfamiliar audience needs. Afterwards he introduced himself as Ted Scott, then the head of the Stanwell Corporation in Queensland. He kindly gave me an unpublished ethics paper he had written and later sent me a gift copy of a short book he and a colleague, Phil Harker, had written, called *Humanity at Work* (1998).

This meeting proved to be a most enriching encounter, for Scott's paper and the book that followed in the mail offered an insight, among plenty of other good things, that greatly encouraged my view of how to motivate for considerate living: the proposal that our dealings with others must either be based on love, or on fear (Scott and Harker 1998: 34ff.). What follows here modifies this insight slightly into the proposal that we all face a choice that defines the kind of person we are, and the kind of life we will build for ourselves, and those we affect. It is the choice whether we will live mainly *for ourselves, or with real, active concern for others as well,* the choice between basically selfish and unselfish ways of relating to others – between generosity and greed.

To explore this great, life-shaping choice, I want to start with the first option, of a life dominated by selfishness. As I do this, we must keep firmly in mind that we as sentient, valorising beings are shaped by a creative desire for the greatest well-being. We must also keep in mind that common sense tells us that the greatest well-being must logically also be long-lasting and sustainable and – crucially – that satisfying this desire depends not only on our own creative efforts, but also on others and their impact on us.

Obviously it is in our interest as individuals to do all we can to encourage others to impact beneficially on us, so we must be very realistic about the extent to which each option will do that. Once we have examined the first option of a selfish choice, we will explore the second choice of generosity in the same way, unpacking what it means in relation to the hunger for well-being and its significant dependence on others for satisfaction.

THE 'ME-FIRST' OPTION OF THE SELFISH

We need to be quite clear about selfishness. It means that someone will subordinate the valid interests of others to his or her own advantage, as a general rule seeking whatever benefits him or her, without much (or even any) concern for anybody else, except when to do so is personally beneficial. It can range from extreme and violent self-interest to milder forms. It is extreme when the person concerned is willing to damage others for his or her own gain, especially if the harm is violent and severe, emotionally or physically – for example, a man beating a woman who is unwilling to do his bidding. Mostly, however, selfishness is milder, stopping short of direct, violent harm to others, while still involving strategies such as subtle control or domination, seldom (if ever) showing any real, active concern to do others good, or thinking much about what they might need.

I remember seeing this kind of milder selfishness in a new member of a cricket team that I captained as a young man. Members were expected to pay a subscription fee, part of which was used to buy basic equipment that could be too expensive for some players. The new person objected to paying the subscription fee, on the grounds that as he had his own kit, he would not be using the club's kit. I thought that this was a selfish attitude, showing lack of concern for others. So, as captain, I pointed out to the new member that he had joined a team and that joining a team meant thinking about and supporting those members who could not afford their own expensive gear. Fortunately, he saw the point, paid up with some initial grumbling, and in the end, became a fine team member.

There is an important difference between selfishness and a valid concern for one's own interests, such as one's health, education, career prospects, hobbies and possessions, and I want to argue that having these concerns is not only natural, but also ethically good. Here we need to be especially honest about ourselves. By nature, each of us is a lifelong sentient being. We feel our own pains and pleasures, our own pangs of hunger and our own enjoyment of food more acutely than we can empathise with the feelings of others, even those whom we love (though their happiness and their sufferings can certainly cause us to feel great joy or anguish). Each of us has a powerful desire to survive and flourish. Each of us develops personal tastes, preferences and interests, which we all want to satisfy. This is how we are made. It is a given, a brute fact of our make-up. And if we neglect ourselves, damaging our health, or our ability to earn a living and be a useful member of society, we thereby also damage others, not only by becoming a burden to them, but also by decreasing our own ability to contribute to their needs.

What can be right or good about a lack of self-concern that disadvantages others? Conscience-based living means a life of generosity and truthfulness, harming none – including ourselves. This makes it right and good to look after our own personal interests to the extent that we can also be generous towards others. By contrast, self-neglect makes us a drain on the time, money and energy of others, which obviously reduces their well-being. This, quite plainly, is wrong. To promote the common good, we therefore need to be good to ourselves too.

Selfishness is different. It comes about when valid, healthy, ethically sound self-concern changes into a concern for nothing and nobody else in their own right, or for truthfulness. At times, it degenerates even further, as I have already explained, into a willingness to damage others for our own gain, or to lie shamelessly when it suits us.

Of course, here too, there is a natural, inborn basis for such selfish behaviour, especially in that reptilian mind of ours, because it feeds on our love of enjoyment, our dread of pain, our passion to survive, and our drive to maximise our own well-being. Selfish living can, all too clearly, be a promising way to satisfy that drive. But having roots in such fertile soil does not make selfishness inevitable. Our natural hunger for well-being says nothing about what to value most and how to live in order to survive and flourish. It leaves that for us to explore, discover and choose.

Of this we must be quite clear: our biology makes it natural and inevitable that we will want the greatest well-being. It makes what I have called a valid and necessary self-concern a natural part of how we function. But biology does not predestine us to selfishness like some almighty genetic god lurking in every cell in our bodies (Hamer 2004: 56ff.). Biology, as we saw when looking at the evidence of brain science, equips us instead for decisions about how to pursue the well-being we are programmed to want. All the same, we need to face up to the biological power of selfishness. Our reptilian brain is an evolutionary success story. In its basic design, it has survived the destructive challenges of millions of years, precisely because it sends such powerful impulses to look after our own needs of food, water, safety and sex.

Once again, Ashbrook and Albright are helpful here in drawing attention to the way the upper brain stem gives rise to highly conservative behaviours and a strong territorial sense. The former maximises survival by limiting activity to what has been found to work in meeting basic needs. Note that this leaves little or no room for learning or adapting to new situations – hence the need for a specific, familiar space or territory. So the dinosaurs perished when their habitat perished. So Hitler and his ilk perished with the destruction of the world they made for themselves by means of force and terror, and so in nature, the crocodile thrives only where crocodiles have always thrived – in warm swamps, sunny sandbanks and rivers. As a result, human society can be seen to have an interest in civilising the tendencies of the reptilian brain – tendencies towards impersonal sexuality and aggression, behaviour that runs on 'automatic pilot' and deception (Ashbrook and Albright 1997: 64ff.).

In mammals, and especially in the human mammal, the reptilian brain is balanced by the other two brain structures that we noted in Chapter Two. These favour what experts sometimes call 'prosocial' behaviour, where wider concerns than self-interest take place, so letting us curb and even transcend the drives of the reptilian brain – should we so choose (Levy 2004; Ridley 1997). If we do not make this choice, selfishness very easily becomes rampant, not only in the individual, but in entire societies. Many of us fear that this is exactly what has happened in the USA in the early years of the twenty-first century because those in control there seem obsessed with their own view of international matters. What is political unilateralism, but another name for selfishness? What is strong-arm politics, but another name for bullying those weaker than you, a favourite tactic of the selfishly strong?

What effect do selfish people have on the rest of us? Here I make an assumption based firstly on a certain amount of fairly hard evidence to the effect that criminally unethical people are a small minority of the adult population in every society, and secondly on my own experience of people. Most people are definitely not habitually selfish, and especially not grossly and violently so, but neither are the numbers of the selfish so trivial that we don't need to worry about them and what they do.

In all of us, there lurks a potential for selfishness that comes into effect from time to time, even if it is of the milder kind, such as just wanting to get our own way. In some of us, it goes up a notch or two, and becomes more serious and longer lasting. But in the main, I have found that most of those with whom I have had contact are basically good people who will lend a hand when needed, keep promises, tell the truth (usually in a kindly way if hard things need to be said), and never deliberately harm others. A select few strike me as being quite saintly, and a few more strike me as being the kind of selfish, self-centred, greedy person I am discussing here.

What effect do the latter have on the rest of us, the generally upright majority of ordinary, decent people? How do we react to people who damage us, break promises, deceive for their own gain, or tell lies? We no longer trust them and may never do so again. We lose respect for them, often permanently. How do we respond to those who control or dominate us, frustrating our natural desire for self-expression and freedom? Most often, we react with mounting resentment and anger, giving them the minimum amount of compliance, and at times, only as much truthfulness as we think we can get away with.

Those whom we see regularly demeaning, hurting or exploiting others, we quickly come to despise and avoid. When they behave in this way towards us, we add even greater resentment to our feelings towards them. If the problem persists or worsens, the feelings will intensify into profound contempt and dislike. When there is cruelty or violence, especially when it is sustained, the negative feelings get even stronger and hatred can arise. Then the desire to see such ugliness get its due recompense – the desire for justice and fairness – can give way to a burning desire for revenge. As I have already said, such ugliness seems mercifully rare most of the time (but not always so rare in the life of whole nations). Even so, we need to keep it in mind as we focus now on the more common kind of milder selfishness.

What the selfish forego, in all cases whether mild or gross, is the respect, trust, liking, and the support of the rest of us. Above all, they lose the support of the morally best among us. They may gain cronies, sycophants, fellow-nasties and toadies, but they lose friends in the real sense, people in whom liking goes together with integrity and loyalty, people who will stand by them when the going gets rough, as it does sooner or later for everybody.

This strikes me as a very high and extremely stupid price to pay for one's own gratification because it so clearly means that we are reducing the willingness of those who affect us to benefit us in any significant way. We all need a world where there are Good Samaritans, such as the Hindu couple who came to my assistance all those years ago, but selfishness reduces the likelihood of them being there for us at all, not only by making the selfish person into the very opposite of a Good Samaritan, but especially by demotivating those who do have a concern for others, above all when there is plenty of manifestly selfish behaviour going on around us.

The old South Africa poisoned many of the wells of kindness in exactly this way, but great kindness has remained a feature of many black South Africans. Even so, I was deeply shocked to learn from a black postgraduate student not long ago that when a relative of hers was involved in a car accident and lay there injured, a few locals, also black, rushed to the scene, not to help, but to grab and make off with anything of value they could find. Such is the damage the new South African must repair. Is it alone in this respect?

Self-serving people seem quite blind to what they are doing to themselves – lessening their own long-term well-being by alienating the good will of the people who form part of their relational worlds and whose goodwill is a crucial factor in their own prospects of flourishing. But then this is what excessive, exclusive self-interest does. By its very nature, it makes us over-aware of our own wants and under-aware, or even blind to the reality of others, who increasingly resent what we do, and sooner or later, look for ways to punish us, or get rid of us. Natural human creativity makes it always possible for them to find a way to deal with us and our self-serving behaviour.

As foolish as such selfishness may be, it is hidden from those who do not – and seemingly cannot – see the reality of their effect on others, on whom they partly depend. However, this does not bother the selfish because, for the time being anyway, it delivers exactly what they want: their own gratification. Those of us questing for a more caring and truthful world must be very clear that selfishness often achieves real, if mostly short-term, beneficial results for the selfish. Drawing on powerful pleasure centres in the brain and on the massively successful reptilian brain structure that we all have, as we saw earlier, what else do we expect?

The pleasures of selfish people as they go after their own gratifications are not the only reason that there are such people. Nature has helped them by creating some innate inequalities. Some of us are born with stronger or taller bodies than others, some with greater brainpower. Men tend to be a good deal stronger physically than women. Unfair cultures and individuals creatively exploit these natural imbalances in their own interests, but the biological platform for exploitation comes first from nature itself. Thus there is a ready doorway of opportunity for those who find themselves physically and mentally able to control others for their own benefit. They find that there are satisfactions to be had by taking what they want from others weaker than themselves, by force if necessary.

This is where the work of Ted Scott and Phil Harker is directly relevant since they show very clearly that fear is used by those with a power advantage of some kind to control others. Some of us are strong enough to hurt others and make them fear being hurt again, and some of us in this position use our strength to get what we want from others. Some among us are clever enough to achieve the same result without physical violence, preferring to use subtle, sly manipulations. Either way, the selfish find scope for their ways.

Our strongest drives are linked closely with our passion for enjoyment and our deep aversion to and fear of pain. How then do most of us react, when we find ourselves exploited, controlled, bullied or manipulated by people stronger than ourselves? With love, respect and wholehearted co-operation? Of course not! We may want or even pretend to have these reactions, but deep down, as we have already noted, what most of us would feel is entirely negative, ranging from uneasiness and dislike to outright rage and hatred, always on the lookout for a way out of our captivity and its pains.

Nature may open a way to exploitation by creating inequalities, but nature also opens doors to liberation and justice, by giving all of us creative minds with which to seek out, plan, and enact strategies of opposition, like white ants eating away at the foundations of the selfish bully's world whenever we can. Many abused women look for ways to get out of the clutches of the men who hurt them. Fearful farm or factory workers might repay unfair employers by doing the minimum amount of work they can get away with. And so on. Loyalty and diligence go right out of the window, though the exploited person will often feel driven to pretend otherwise.

For selfishness, the clock of opposition therefore ticks away inexorably, even if the people who live in this way don't hear it. Again, the old South Africa is an excellent example of an entire society governed by the collective selfishness of its former white rulers. Everything was organised to ensure the continued power and benefit of the heavily armed minority of South Africans with European forebears, like me, and to the detriment of all others. The best homes, schools, sports facilities, jobs, universities, medical care and even graveyards were reserved for whites, in addition to the control of and access to the best weapons. Not content with these spoils, there were also white people who added insult to injury with nastily racist attitudes, demeaningly speaking of adult black women as 'girls' and men as 'boys'. I even recall seeing cheap cuts of meat in butchers' shops labelled 'boys' meat' for a white family's black gardener, who might be 50 years old, or more. As I acknowledged earlier in this book, one of those ugly and hurtful ways of speaking even found its way for a while into my own vocabulary many years ago.

How did black South Africans react to this? By forgetting and forgiving the theft of their lands, their independence, their wealth and their dignity, thanking God fervently every night for the blessings of the white man's civilisation, his firm guiding hand, his fiercely balled fist and his trigger-happy index finger? Or by remembering every detail of the daily oppression, never accepting it, keeping alive the dream of freedom, exploring every crevice of opportunity to undo the injustice, and never giving up? We all know which reaction took place, and we all know how it ended, with good at last prevailing over evil, conscience over greed and contempt.

The powerful white minority of the old South Africa, fixated by its own selfish, and indeed *fearful* interests, did not understand that in a relational world such us ours, you cannot damage others and the wider world, without damaging and even, at times, dooming yourself. The world is peopled by creative beings driven by an unquenchable yearning for true well-being, for respect, liberty and happiness, people who do not passively succumb to the sight of guns and the thunder of helicopters overhead. Instead, these people constantly seek ways to undo oppressive power and never give up. Neither, it seems, did Hitler's Germany or Stalin's Soviet Union understand this reality, and neither, worrisomely, it seems, does the USA today, which seems willing to impose its will on the rest of the world by force, if it so chooses.

There are six conclusions to be reached from this exploration of the selfish option. First, choosing to be selfish has enough success in the form of satisfaction and pleasure to make it a real option for clever, powerful individuals and nations, especially in the shorter term. Stupid bullies usually blunder their way to their own downfall quite soon, but cunning ones can keep going for much longer. People of conscience who care about more than only their own interests need to be very realistic about this.

Second, however, the long-term prospects for selfishness are problematic, especially for grossly selfish individuals or groups and for exploitative societies that impose their will cruelly on others. Here is why: their egoistic exploitation, cheating and harming of others makes their victims – for that is what they are – react with resentment, anger, and even hatred. It makes them look for ways to escape, to undermine, to redress, and sometimes to get revenge. This relational world is thus to the selfish a world with many hidden threats, as they alienate, anger and disgust those whom they exploit – particularly the morally best and most creative of their victims. These are people who believe in justice, generosity and integrity, and who use their intelligence and creativity to curb and remove the unjust and the cruel, their willingness to make real sacrifices making them formidable foes.

I have already explained in detail that the well-being that we all want cannot be had without the contribution of others, as much as getting it selfishly by dominating, exploiting and damaging others is clearly a temptation for powerfully selfish people and societies. Provided they buy the support of similarly greedy allies, bribing them with money, privileges and other benefits, and back it up with the ever-present threat of punishment for any who waver or oppose them, the strategy can work, especially in the timescales of a few decades. This is why we see so much of this selfish option. But always, its effect is to alienate others, some of whom will then use their creativity to ally with others to undo those who oppress them. In the end, they tend to win. The world saw this with Hitler's Germany and with other regimes and individuals who went the way of the selfish.

Third, the kind of well-being available to the selfish is generally physical and superficial. Not for them, the self-respect, esteem and genuine friendship of the finest people – people of courage, integrity, fairness and generosity of both spirit and action towards all – that many of us find much more meaningful than mere physical enjoyments. Not for them, the sense of deep worth that comes from finding yourself capable of real and costly sacrifice for someone else. This shows that selfishness cannot yield *maximal* well-being, even in the short term. Logical analysis shows it to be sub-optimal. It cannot deliver the deepest experiences of enrichment available to us as humane beings, and above all, it is unlikely to last for very long.

Fourth, alas, these inherent limitations of the selfish option are seldom seen by the selfish. If their upbringing and surrounding culture have deprived them of deeper, richer experiences and fostered in them a love of selfish, instant gratifications, they will want them more than anything else. Here too, people of conscience need to understand the kind of adversary their quest for a more humane world will encounter, and must transform.

Fifth, for those of us who want a more caring world, this situation creates a very serious challenge: to work ethically for a change of heart and mind in the selfish and reduce the space available for them – something I will explore in Chapter Five, which deals with ways of enhancing the power of conscience in ourselves and our world.

The sixth lesson is that the people of the USA, especially, are now living in a time of crucial trial, what Christians sometimes call a 'kairos moment' from the biblical idea of a time of critical decision. Will they turn back from the politics of national selfishness, and rather go for the good of the world *as defined by the world*, and *not only by the White House*, or plunge further from their own democratic ideals, at great and perhaps disastrous cost to themselves, to all of us, and to conscience itself? The many people in that great country who are committed to a world of friendship need all the support and resources that we in the rest of the world who share a commitment to maximal well-being can give them.

This book tries to do exactly that. The next stage in this chapter is to explain why the option for considerate, shared ways of using power throughout the world is the one that will win in the end.

EXPLORING THE OPTION OF INCLUSIVE CONCERN

Turning now to the other option – the choice of generosity – let me again start the exploration by explaining the kind of lifestyle I have in mind when I speak of a life where there is active concern for others. We are not talking about self-denial or self-sacrifice in the strong and heroic sense of those rare individuals who give up the pleasures and pursuits of normal life in order to serve others. One of the best examples that I have experienced of such people came in a grim, poor area of London's East End during my student days.

I was new in England and as yet, had no family or friends there with whom I could spend the wintry Christmas period. So my wise and kindly tutor at Oxford arranged for me to stay in a modest guest room at a monastic community of a group of Anglican Franciscans called the House of the Divine Compassion. For a fortnight, I saw daily something of the lives of these people, dedicated to community work, social service, drug rehabilitation and poverty relief, done selflessly and with unfailing good cheer.

Life was frugal and the heating minimum, but the warmth of their commitment more than made up for these small hardships. None of the brothers struck me as the type that could not cope with ordinary life and therefore takes to the cloister for refuge. I saw them as strong personalities, some of them highly educated, who would have excelled in the outside world. Yet there they were, with their vows of poverty, chastity and obedience, giving everything for their faith in the great Franciscan tradition of loving service for the needy and the rejected.

Such moral heroism fills me with something close to awe. It is also something I know that I could not match. There is too much of the hedonist, the lover of life's enjoyments in me for that, and, I suspect, in most others. So for the rest of us, the majority who are not moral gold medallists at the Ethics Olympics, the crossbar must be set lower. For us, it is a matter of *combining due self-concern with an active concern for the well-being of others – at times requiring a measure of real sacrifice from us.* It means having a spirit of generosity that leads to acts of kindness involving our time, talents, efforts and resources, especially for those who are innocently in trouble. It means never intentionally harming others. It also means being a truthful person, for benefit depends ultimately on truth, not falsehood (by which I mean both indifference to truth and outright lying, not what is sometimes called a 'white lie') except in very rare situations where telling the truth will harm an innocent person – something that is explored in Chapter Four in connection with truthfulness. By living this way, we strike a balance of concern for others and for ourselves, and we can become good examples, and reliable, honourable members of families, teams, workplace situations, nations, and indeed, the world.

In people like this, I see an inner goodness that wins my unqualified admiration and that is surely its own reward. But what of their impact on those whom they influence and on their own desire for an enjoyable life? How do we as ordinary people who are neither saints nor villains react to the presence of those who show the kind of actively inclusive concern and integrity we are exploring?

Here too readers, like my audiences, need to think about their own experience and heed it. What I find from my experience and from the replies of my audiences is a wealth of positive reactions. We find that the example set by good and decent people wins our respect and admiration. All of us will feel appreciation for the way that their lives enhance our well-being. We then find ourselves willing to help and support such people. Where their levels of manifest concern and integrity are high, they win loyalty, and even devotion from us.

Thus they put real, humane power into the relational world, investing it with their generosity of spirit and action, their truthfulness, and their refusal to cause harm. And when they err, as we all do, even if in mostly quite minor ways, we feel even more respect if they face their own shortcomings honestly, and seek to make amends for any hurt caused. When a large majority of people in any group – from family to nation – lives in this way, the result is a context where the prospects of maximum well-being are greatly enhanced because, as experience shows, integrity, trustworthiness and supportiveness, even from total strangers, are generally there. Levels of fear decline, confidence rises, effort and energy are released in worthy ways. More and more of us, as we experience the benefits and the satisfactions of such contexts, strengthen them even further with our loyalty and commitment, so increasing the prospects of long-lasting well-being.

Best of all, perhaps, life's richest and deepest experiences become possible: real friendship, profound respect, powerful feelings of loyalty and the kind of love that is only possible when these other feelings are also present, at times a love so strong that those whose lives are filled with it will make costly sacrifices and even, however rarely, lay down their own lives for others. So important is the love that I have in mind as a motivator of ethical living that I make the generosity from which it springs central to my account of the main moral values in Chapter Four.

Brain science is once more very revealing about our built-in equipment for altruistic behaviour, and again, Ashbrook and Albright highlight it very helpfully. They explain that the most recently evolved part of the mammalian brain gives rise to powers no reptile has, especially in connection with care for the young (1997: 78, 84). Of course, human babies are exceptionally vulnerable and utterly dependent on such care, while their mothers need support during pregnancy, and in the early months and years after giving birth. In humanity's hugely long period of being hunter-gatherers, this dependency would have been acute, as it sometimes is even today for poor single mothers. They need a partner who will not walk off in search of an unencumbered female at this time, a partner not governed by his reptilian mind, but his mammalian and – dare we say it – human mind. The mammalian brain and the cortex provide for such abilities, but this does not make them in the least bit inevitable. So we have to foster them. Conscience aims to do exactly that. Crucially, the brain cannot even develop properly without what Ashbrook and Albright call 'an empathetic caregiver' (1997: 84).

All of this calls into serious doubt the idea, so beloved by many right-wing economic and political theorists that we humans are by nature incorrigibly selfish beings. The truth is that by nature, we are ambivalent creatures, equipped for both egoism and concern for others – and for choosing between them, and so too, are entire societies and the many organisations that they contain.

We can now also see exactly why *genuine* democracies are more stable than dictatorships. Nations that organise themselves for the benefit of all are manifestly and inherently more likely to thrive – to produce the greatest well-being for the longest time – than the attempt to corner power and profit for a favoured few. This is because *genuinely* democratic nations have a strong, built-in tendency to maximise loyalty, stability and productivity. It is no different when it comes to organising an entire world.

It can also be asked at this point why – if democracy is indeed so desirable – it did not emerge earlier in human history. The answer is that great differences of power come naturally, as we have already seen: men being generally stronger than women, some men stronger than others, some people more intelligent than others, and humans more powerful than any other species. The strong, especially where education and insight are minimal, might easily see this reality as a way to control others, and some do exactly that. Enter the long line of lion kings and the alpha males. It takes time to mobilise the resources of mind, heart and action to spread a new message about sharing power equally. The world has not got there yet, but few people who have heard it reject this message, apart from the minority that it threatens. In short, only in recent centuries have societies begun to reach conditions favourable to the birth of genuine democracy (unlike the very minimal democracy of ancient Greece).

This is the truth that must be taken deeply to heart by those presently controlling the USA, because they alone have the power to facilitate a genuine move away from tyranny and towards the common good of the planet – *to facilitate and not impose it* – for you cannot impose goodness, respect or love, or any of life's finest fruits. But is this not asking too much of any nation, that it find ways to serve both its own interests and those of other nations?

It can be argued that group loyalties such as patriotism probably have a biological base, so that it goes against the grain of human nature to expect US citizens, or anybody else, to overcome them. Here is why I disagree with this objection. It cannot be denied that nations and cultural communities, as a matter of fact, seem to put their own interests, as they see them, above the interests of others. They are where we feel at home, and therefore we will feel loyalty towards our communities and nations, while most others strike us as more or less alien and even – though we seldom say this out loud – in some ways, inferior. So it can indeed seem natural that national self-interest will prevail over international co-operation as a better way to serve the interests of its members.

Nationalism and cultural identities and the loyalties they create must be accepted as powerful realities. But this does not make them immovable, or part of an unchangeable human biology, unlike our common human nature, which has been stable over countless millennia, like our drive for happiness. Instead, they must be seen as *artefacts*, not brute facts of nature set everlastingly in concrete. Over time, they come and go, and are always, in principle, open to change by human effort. In the mid-1800s, there was such a thing as Prussian nationalism; now it is history, removed by the changes that the Germans made to their homeland. At the same time, the southern states of today's USA were part of a separate confederation, with a very deep sense of loyalty and identity as a slave-owning culture. This has long gone because people such as Abraham Lincoln, and the many who rallied to his anti-slavery cause, took steps to end it. In Imperial Russia, there was loyalty to the czar, and in the USSR to Marxism-Leninism. These are also gone, probably forever – brought to an end by people such as Lenin and Gorbachev, respectively.

The argument of this book is that global well-being must rest on something much more basic and durable than these slowly shifting accidents of nationhood and culture, massively powerful though they are at given stages of human existence – just as tribal identities once were for all people. I have sought a stronger foundation in the abiding, basic realities of a common human nature, the same for all people at all times, with its passion for well-being, and its awesome creative ability for good and ill, and in the interrelatedness of all things. I see no evidence that biology makes us overridingly loyal to whatever nation or culture we are part of. What I do see in the evidence is that our biology does make us form very deep bonds *of some kind*. A social species such as ours, with all its individual vulnerabilities, would not survive if biology gave it no more than the drives of the reptilian brain to self-serving behaviours. It must therefore also have a built-in tendency towards strong bonds with others, which create loyalty and a sense of identity. This much must be granted. But what those bonds are, and what we are loyal to, is cultural. It can be changed by creative human effort, by education and by exposure to the good in other nations and cultures. It is an artefact, not a prevailing given.

As individuals, we all have experiences of changing ties and loyalties. Some of us leave the countries where we were raised to study or live elsewhere, gradually finding our hearts at home in a new country. We may leave behind one religious bond for another, or develop new loves and friendships, and so on.

None of this changes, except the timescales, when we move to the level of nations and entire cultures. The USA and other powerful nations can do as they please and suffer no adverse consequences in the short term, but the hurt inflicted on other parts of the world will not go away, and will work against their interests by fostering long-term forces of opposition whose day will come. This may not bother those too old, selfish or short-sighted to care, but it should bother those who think carefully and understand that genuine moral commitment is not disheartened by the fact that moral power sometimes takes a long time to make itself felt, and those who care about the kind of world their children and grandchildren will live in. Do they really want a world where their citizens and those who work for their corporations around the globe are fair game for networks of terrorists seething with anger at decades of domination, and where their products and companies are shunned in favour of those of its competitors by decent people who have had enough of this new and global kind of imperialism?

It will be very clear now what the answer is to the question thrust upon us by our ambivalent surrounding world. Which way of living is more likely to yield greater and more durable well-being? Is it the manipulative, and at times, forcibly domineering way of the selfish person that we can all be, and which some of us have let ourselves be, or even have chosen to be? Or is it the alternative of showing due and active concern both for our own honourable interests and for those whom we affect?

Anybody who can think logically and who is not captive to self-interest and its limited – although still very real – pleasures, will see that the life of active, inclusive concern, which includes moral integrity, is inherently more likely to foster the greatest, sustainable well-being, which is a very far cry from superficial pleasure. This brings me to the last and shortest, but culminating part of in my case for ethical living.

INCLUSIVE CONCERN AS THE WAY OF CONSCIENCE

Earlier in this book, I defined a life of conscience as a life marked at heart by genuine, active generosity, harmlessness and truthfulness. In this chapter, the goal has been to give an answer to those who ask why anybody would want to live in this way, rather than simply living for their own satisfaction, backing it up with evidence from science and the history of morality.

Central to my answer is the appeal to our natural human drive for the greatest and longest lasting well-being. I have used this crucial reality to show that in our relational world, a life of inclusive concern is much better equipped to yield the positive experiences and stable situations that we all want for ourselves and those who matter most to us (ideally for all human beings) than a life of mere self-interest. This is why it makes sense to the informed and logical mind to choose the former, the life of inclusive concern. Now that we see why selfishness undermines itself, especially in the long run, we need to explore the main values that flow from a rich, transformed conscience – the subject of the next chapter.

CONCLUDING SUMMARY OF MY ARGUMENT SO FAR

- Why would an intelligent person with a strong drive for well-being want to show active concern for others as well? Why be altruistic or delay gratification? I have argued that concern for others is the intelligent option because it is unwise not to invest effort in our long-term prospects of having the fulfilled life that everybody by nature wants.

- In addition, kindness, respect, honesty, and a refusal to harm make the surrounding world of people, places and nature, *on which our own well-being significantly depends*, a happier, safer and more productive world, with greater potential for fulfilment than a resentful, fearful and hostile world.

- My case for considerate living appeals to natural factors, both human and environmental, rather than supernatural factors. The religious appeal to these factors has given rise to a widespread belief that morality has been benignly bestowed on a sinfully reluctant humanity for its own good by a God or some other divine power. Christians, for example, believe that nature is a fallen thing, shot through with evil and needing divine help, which it gets from Christ and the Bible. Because this belief is confined to only one of the world's value-systems, like all religious beliefs, neither it nor any other such view of why we should care about others can work for all of humanity.

- Nor can we find the necessary, globally inclusive grounds for unselfish living in Western moral philosophy, though the reasoning skills it provides are an important part of my argument for a life of generosity, rather than one based on greed and selfishness. It is too Western, too abstract, and too ineffective in practice to inspire the world to a more caring way of life.

- Openness to all on an equal footing seems to me, after the horrors of apartheid and Auschwitz, to be a non-negotiable ethical priority, so I have had to turn elsewhere for an answer to those who, quite reasonably, ask why we should care much about anything other than our own interests. This does not mean that I reject religious views of ethics, only that they cannot do the inclusive motivational job that has to be done if we are to create an effective global conscience, as I believe we must.

- So I turn to nature and human nature in ways that we can all explore, finding there the roots and kinds of evil – harm, violence, selfishness, lies – that religions also say disfigure nature and humanity, but also finding in human nature, the roots of great human goodness.

- In human nature, we find what philosophers of science call the necessary initial conditions for good and evil. We live in a relational universe and a relational world where all things interrelate, sometimes benefiting us, and sometimes harming us. This means that if anything as vulnerable and fragile as a living organism is to survive and thrive, it must adapt to that ambivalence, attuning itself to sources of benefit, and trying to avoid sources of harm.

- We humans, embedded in such a world, come into it equipped with a powerful, valorising drive, rich with feeling, seeking the greatest well-being and with immense creative potential and freedom to make the necessary adaptations to our ambivalent home by finding and embracing whatever leads to the benefits we seek.

- The way the world works triggers in us tentative value-seeking behaviours, through which we are on the lookout always to find out, by trial and error, what brings benefits, which we naturally approve of and call good.

- Experience further teaches us that some of these goods are richer and more satisfying than others, none more so than a freely chosen commitment to care actively for others, as well as for ourselves. Experience further shows that there are pleasurable satisfactions to be had from living selfishly, especially for those of us with the strength and cunning to exploit others.

- The findings of modern brain science lead me to the following way of summarising our human condition in relation to ethics. From our reptilian minds, we get messages such as, 'Food now! Water now!' and – more ominously – 'Sex now!' From our mammalian minds, we hear different messages, such as 'Food is better enjoyed when shared. Sex is better when enfolded by love, faithfulness and respect for the partner.' And from our distinctively human brain structures in the neocortex, comes a third message, inviting us to choose what we will be: selfish or caring. What is all of this, if not a verified, nature-based explanation of conscience and why it works so superbly for some, but not (yet) for all?

- The pressure on us to survive and thrive is very great, meaning that we cannot afford to put much effort into behaviours that do not help us achieve those two key goals. But the evidence of history and our own experience is clear: humanity everywhere puts massive energies into a quest for good, and does so *because it works in practice, delivering more and better long-lasting well-being than harmful and deceitful behaviours.*

- The ethical way is therefore the wiser and more productive option for a world of well-being. It exists to foster the beneficial power of our passions for fulfilment, freedom and self-assertion in an interrelated world with many inequalities, and to counter their destructive potential.

four

Values for Greater Global Flourishing

Imagine the following conversation between two young women who are discussing abortion, which is now legal in many countries. They both want to live responsible, caring lives, but for different reasons. One of them thinks abortion is ethically right, while the other disagrees. The latter is a devout Roman Catholic, and she argues that from conception onwards, we are unique human beings, already infused with immortal souls, so that abortion means murder. Her friend, who turns to human rights for her values, and not to religion, replies that medical science has now shown that this belief cannot be true because in the very earliest stage of pregnancy, the embryo can develop into twins or triplets, and therefore at this early stage, we don't yet have a unique human being, according to this view. She adds that the embryo is just tissue, so that expelling it is no different, really, from removing any other part of the mother's body, like donating a kidney. This evokes the reply that genetics has shown this idea to be false, for the embryo is not just like any other part of the mother's tissue; it is genetically unique. So how can it be up to the mother or anybody else to dispose of it in the way she might donate a kidney or bone marrow?

We are all now citizens of the 'Information Age'. We are heirs to a vast body of new knowledge that has changed the world and important parts of our own lives, such as medical care, communication, computers and travel. But at the same time, there are other aspects of life that have been far less exposed to new knowledge. One such aspect is conscience. For vast numbers of people, it remains firmly embedded in philosophy and in religions, where continuity with their own founding events and traditions, rather than creativity, is the norm. This means that their values have little real exposure to one another. Many traditional believers and leaders therefore see no great need to open their windows to the winds of change blowing across the world in the form of conscience.

This is a mistake. Knowledge is power, and power needs to be directed by conscience, lest it be driven by greed and the desire to dominate. Even more important, *conscience itself needs power – humane power – in order to make a real difference, and knowledge is a key part of that power.*

Experience shows us that human goodness does not need much information to be effective in our immediate dealings with others, but conscience nonetheless grows in depth, strength and extent when it is well informed. A well-informed conscience is essential for tackling our problems in ways that lead to greater global and local well-being.

This chapter therefore provides information about the core values that are essential if there is to be greater flourishing in a rapidly globalising world. It has three main sections. We will start with the experience of deep moral value, and then turn to the set of core moral values that I see as the marks of a rich, global conscience, noting also the evils that undermine these values. In order to do this inclusively, I will refer back to human nature, in order to see which values are logically needed for the greatest well-being. The third part of this chapter is an overview of the world's main ethical traditions and how they have arisen. This too, is essential, if we are to have a global ethic.

There are several reasons for including this third category of information. First, most people take their moral bearings from these great spiritual traditions and always have, so we must respect them by seeking sensitivity and insight into them. Second, most people have very little or even no knowledge of traditions other than their own, making it nigh impossible for them to relate to people from other cultural backgrounds in an informed way. Third, we need to see that the set of values discussed in this chapter matches the moral wisdom of those traditions, a fact that gives the world a very important, though not universal, basis for building a shared global conscience. Thus this chapter aims to give readers what they need to know about the domain of conscience in our time of cultural pluralism, burgeoning knowledge and globalisation.

DEEP ETHICAL VALUE

Turning now to the first part of the knowledge about good and evil covered in this chapter, let me invite readers to travel with me back to an experience of deep ethical value. I will relate the following story that I heard a few years ago when visiting South Africa's infamous Robben Island, where Nelson Mandela and many others were imprisoned under apartheid.

Our guide that day had been a prisoner on Robben Island. He showed us the limestone quarry where prisoners were made to work, telling us about the cruelties and gross indignities visited by some of the warders on their charges. He also explained how the better-educated prisoners would pass on their knowledge to those with little schooling.

And then, as I recall, he told our group a story that affected me deeply. After an episode of sheer nastiness by one of the warders, a number of the leading prisoners gathered and vowed that when the new, democratic South Africa came, it would transcend the cruelty and injustice of the old one. It would not be a place of retribution and vengeance, but of justice and reconciliation. This was the only way that apartheid could be truly defeated, and is now being defeated and transcended through the rich consciences and commitments of people like that group of unbowed captives (see Gobodo-Madikizela 2003).

Next, I invite readers to think of similar experiences of their own and recall what they felt and thought. Maybe it was the generosity of a surprise overseas holiday arranged and paid for by their children. Maybe it was a small boy's spontaneous act of kindness to a beggar. Maybe there are readers who also remember Martin Luther King Jr.'s 'I have a dream' speech (Carson 1999: 223–227) and feel its power to this day. Everybody will have several such experiences to recall, maybe even many. It is these experiences that will show us what deep ethical value means.

Returning now to what I heard on Robben Island, the reactions that I experienced are as follows. I felt moved and inspired at such nobility of soul. I felt more than simple admiration for those men; I felt awe, suffused with deep gratitude. I was uplifted and enriched, and I still feel these emotions when I recall that day. So too, when I think back to Martin Luther King Jr.'s great speeches, and when I think of the way that Socrates and Christ went so unforgettably to their deaths, or of moments of family life that were wonderfully good, pouring into my life rich and long-lasting energy for worthwhile living. I look back on these and other experiences as landmark events, as peak experiences of sheer goodness. I have no doubt that others have had them too, and that they had the same kind of reaction.

Mindful of these reactions, let us turn now to asking ourselves why we react as we do to these experiences. What makes these events and the people involved so special, so richly meaningful, and so powerful? What gives them such great value? I see four main features that figure strongly in all the moments of great upliftment that have happened to me: generosity, cost, self-transcendence and rarity.

The group of Robben Island political prisoners that vowed to build a better South Africa were not committing themselves to furthering their own personal interests, but to the good of all, including the good of the whites who had so relentlessly oppressed them. This meant vowing to devote their coming freedom to nation building, giving it their time, passion and effort. Notice the word *giving* in the previous sentence – a sure sign that generosity of spirit, purpose, and ultimately, action are present. The same is true of Martin Luther King Jr., as he gave inspired leadership to the civil rights movement in the USA, a generation ago, to those in Australia who work for justice for its Aboriginal people, and also to the South Africans who resisted apartheid. The same is certainly true of that Indian couple who helped me to hospital all those years ago.

What all these people did came at a cost to them, sometimes a very great cost. In the end, Martin Luther King Jr. paid with his life for his stand against racism, but long before that, there were many other sacrifices, perhaps above all, foregoing an easier life of getting on with a career and normal family life.

I see no wrong in wanting a normal, easier life. It is the path that most of us as ordinary, good people choose. But when somebody decides to give it up for a larger cause that can benefit many others, then there is great cost involved and we feel deep admiration, and even awe at such people. The Indian couple who helped me after I came off my motor scooter could have hurried on with their day's work, as others who passed by did. Instead they gave of their time and resources, and ignored the law about segregated taxis, choosing the more difficult option, not the easy one – and all for a member of the oppressive community.

Even greater was the cost to those political prisoners on South Africa's Robben Island. Nelson Mandela spent 27 years of his life as a prisoner, most of them there. Many others served very long sentences there. Steve Biko paid with his life, after a terrible beating by agents of the apartheid regime. These individuals and their loved ones paid an enormous price for the rest of us, a debt for which many feel an undying awe and gratitude.

Along with generosity and cost, experiences of deep value also involve what we could call self-transcendence. The selfish option, which comes naturally enough as we saw in the previous chapter, is overridden. The easy option, the safe and comfortable option, is bypassed and a choice made for something harder and less comfortable, even dangerous, for the sake of others. The part of us that looks after our own personal interests, our own preservation and safety, is reined in and the part of us that cares actively for others takes over. The cortex and mammalian brain transcend the reptilian mind in what I see as one of life's most wonderful realities – the ability to hear the call of a good greater than our own, to answer it and become one with it. Small wonder that religious people sense in this reality not only the power of self-transcendence – of people choosing to lift themselves to a higher plane in answer to the call of a higher reality than self-interest – but also the presence of some kind of divine transcendence.

The fourth feature of these experiences of deep value is their rarity. In the material world, things tend to rise in value when they are scarce, like water in the desert. I see the landscape of conscience as a pleasant land of gentle, rolling hills representing ordinary human goodness. Here and there, the hillsides show signs of fires. Here and there along the roads, we find mishaps and accidents, sometimes fatal ones. These represent the evils that disfigure that pleasant landscape. And on the horizon, there is a range of mountains with a few great and glorious peaks. The fact that they are few adds to their beauty.

I have marvelled at the lovely majesty of Mont Blanc in France, Mount Cook in New Zealand and Mount Whitney in the USA, and I suspect that their beauty would be less striking if they were flanked by scores of identical peaks. Rarity does seem to add value and when we find something uniquely beautiful or good, the value becomes much greater. I suspect that something like this is also true of life's special times of deep value, giving them the ability to stand out like shimmering mountain-tops of light and hope.

Best of all, perhaps, each one of us can be that rare and precious mountain-top of kindness, courage and truthfulness. This is a key truth about conscience that we all need to understand. It was brought home to me vividly after a keynote address I had given at a conference of radical religious believers in New Zealand a few years ago. In my address, I had explained that my approach to ethics was from the ground up, based on experience, not from the heavens down. I added that I had not been on some Mount Sinai, some holy mountain of moral revelation. After my address a man came up to me and said that he had just one disagreement with me. He said, 'You *are* on the holy mountain. *You* are the holy mountain. We are *all* the holy mountain.' What he meant is that peak experiences of really deep value may be rare over the course of a life, but they are the gift and privilege of each one of us as equal citizens of the commonwealth of conscience.

With this important and liberating truth in our minds and hearts, we can now turn to the essential values of a shared ethic, values that foster greater well-being for a world with far too many sorrows.

NINE CORE VALUES FOR A WORLD OF WELL-BEING

In Chapter Three, I presented my case that we have an inborn drive for the greatest well-being, and that we are equipped with brain structures adapted to that drive. We also saw that in a relational world, the enjoyments and satisfactions we seek cannot be had in isolation from others because they depend to a significant extent on the goodwill of those around us, and on the resources of nature.

All of this is a 'given' – a set of realities within which we must live as natural, biological beings. What is not a given, but must be learnt anew by everybody in each succeeding generation, is what to value most and how to manage life on the basis of those values, so that we use our creativity beneficially and not harmfully. As such, we are cultural beings – creators of and heirs to patterns of living that depend on education, not genes, in order to move from brain to brain, mind to mind, heart to heart, and generation to generation. We also saw in Chapter Three that the path of active concern for others – the ethical path of conscience – is inherently more likely to lead to the enhanced well-being that we all want than to the opposite path, the path of exploitation and control, especially in the long term.

What, then, are the values that must be practised if we as individuals and communities are to experience the deepest well-being? What does a lifestyle of care and concern involve? I find it useful at this point to ask myself what kind of person I need to be if I am to be a source of benefit to others, an agent, as moral philosophers would say, of beneficence. What kind of character is needed in all of us if we are to be people who make goodness happen? My analysis of the logical requirements of the greatest possible well-being produces a set of nine essential values: generosity, integrity, truthfulness, respect, justice and fairness, inclusiveness, responsible effort in the service of the good, freedom governed by responsibility, and beauty of presence.

Heart and mind working together

Before we go through these core values, we need to be clear about the way heart and mind work together in the domain of conscience. As we set our hearts on interests wider than our own, we also need to get our minds right about our moral concerns. It is possible to think of conscience and the ethical living that it inspires as having two main sets of values, those of beneficence and those of truthfulness, so long as we keep in mind that they work together in our daily lives.

Moral goodness, as I have now often emphasised, means caring about the good of others, as well as taking due care of our own legitimate interests. But who exactly are these 'others'? We see at once that for conscience to work, we need to know and understand what we are to care about. So a commitment to truth, to sound knowledge, is immediately part and parcel of human goodness.

Who then are these others? What must we understand about them? We must understand that they and all people are basically just like us because of our shared human nature. This truth we discover best by interacting with one another, sharing our stories and coming to sense and appreciate our shared humanity. Not that we are all the same in all respects; equality is a deeper reality than that. It means that everybody has feelings, basic needs, a desire for happiness and sense of self-worth or dignity. Each of us is utterly unique. Each of us values life itself and wants to preserve and protect it. Each of us can give and receive love. We need to see very clearly that none us stands higher than others in terms of our basic humanity in these crucial aspects of life.

We also need to understand that in a relational world where life and well-being are togetherness things, each of us also needs a supportive context. This is why I emphasised context in Chapter One and relationality in Chapter Two. Nobody can truly thrive in families, schools, workplaces and nations marked by violence, fear and disorder. For generosity of spirit and action to be effective, it must be more than a desire for the well-being of each person. It must also be a desire that each person will live in the kind of social context and natural environment that sustains, rather than undermines or damages.

But if it is no more than an idea in our heads, then knowledge of the principle of equality, of human nature and the vital importance of supportive contexts is not good enough – because ethical living is all about *making goodness happen*. What is in our minds therefore needs the activating power of the human heart to care about those others and to want their fulfilment and happiness. Beneficence is at once a quality of mind and of heart.

It is a pity that in English and other Western languages, we have separate words like heart and head, feelings and minds, values and facts, because in practice, the two are so closely intertwined as to function as one reality, as we will see. We lack a term for this combination. I have been told that the Chinese are better off in this regard because they have a single concept, heart-mind. What I am therefore going to do is follow the Chinese and explain the core moral values of both heart and mind in tandem and then, at the end, express them as two sets: those of beneficence and those of truthfulness.

THE NINE CORE VALUES

What follows does not pretend to capture all the world's ethical wealth, for one of the most important lessons that we learn by exploring the wonderful world of conscience is just how much greater it is than even the best we can be and understand. So I have a much more modest goal for what follows, namely to offer what I have found in order to encourage readers to do the same with their own experience. In the sphere of conscience, in the moral domain, the least of us, as judged by the norms of a status-crazy world, is a sovereign, with a wealth of ethical experience to draw from, explore and share. Thus readers may come up with additional values, or give greater prominence to some values than I do, or have longer or shorter sets than mine.

Why does my list of core values have nine items? There is nothing morally significant about the number, but there definitely is practical value in having a set of core values that is short enough to be memorised, but not so short that it becomes too general.

The nine values are all positive ones. They show us what to embrace, not what to avoid. It is very important that we get away from any idea that ethics is mostly a negative series of 'don'ts' whose effect is to make life cheerless. The truth is the very opposite, for the whole point even of the taboos and prohibitions is to make life richer and more deeply enjoyable for as many people as possible.

At the same time, we must also avoid the trap of being naive. Evil is a reality that must be faced, understood and transcended. To help this happen, the discussion of core values that follows includes the opposites of these values, the gang of evils that we most need to overcome.

Generosity

Generosity is fundamental to a life governed by conscience. It means wanting things to be well with others; it means being willing to give what we can to further their well-being, and it means never intentionally harming or injuring them. Thus it brings to our lives a basic orientation or policy that leads us to generous action.

We also need to understand that being a generous person, a person with a heart, can express itself in different ways in relation to the needs of those with whom we have contact, but it is always with a feeling of concern for their good. For somebody in pain or suffering, it takes the form of compassion, care and help. For the weak or defenceless, it means protection. To those near and dear to us, it manifests as love. Towards those for whom things are going well, for colleagues and associates, it means friendship, supportiveness and loyalty. For those whose situations we do not know, it takes the form of courtesy, and so on. Towards ourselves, if generosity is ethical and not just self-indulgence, it expresses itself as due concern for our basic needs and for as much flourishing as possible without harm or disadvantage to others, particularly without intentional harm. To the future selves that we hope to become, generosity means looking beyond immediate concerns and investing effort and resources sensibly for the days ahead.

Thus a single moral value turns into a rich spectrum of expressions, just as a prism splits light into a lovely range of colours. It also brings to mind some memorable words that I found in the book by Scott and Harker that I mentioned in previous chapters. They quote Winston Churchill as saying: 'We make a living by what we get. We make a life by what we give' (1998: 119). We humans may be the result of a long and relentless process of evolution, where life feeds violently on life in order to survive, or we may be flawed by an ingrained selfishness that many Christians see as original sin. Either way, the reality of a world where this great and noble quality of generosity is present should inspire and uplift us all. This wonderful human ability to receive life from others can be treated as a gift and made a source for our own ways of giving.

In traditions governed by faith in a divine creator, generosity is elevated to the pinnacle of value by being seen as the very heart of a deity, who creates the universe as an act of pure generosity and love. As a former Bishop of Durham and a teacher of mine at Oxford, David Jenkins, wrote at the start of his book *Living with Questions*, 'God is either a gift or a delusion' (1969: ix). These same faiths also tell us that divine generosity does not exhaust itself by creating the universe, but also expresses itself in the gifts of guidance, sacred revelations and, according to Christianity, in the person of Christ and the coming of the Holy Spirit. While these traditions differ about where they find divine generosity, they all agree that it is supremely real.

This brings me to explore a word related to generosity – magnanimity – following a verbal suggestion from my colleague, Munyaradzi Murove. Tracking the ancestry of this word proves to be very revealing. It comes from two Latin words meaning 'great soul'. It is thus the exact equivalent of the title given in India and now by the whole world to Gandhi, for 'Mahatma' has exactly the same meaning. It is also said to have been a characteristic of Muhammed. Many in South Africa and around the world see the same quality in Nelson Mandela.

We should avoid the danger of thinking that magnanimity is something we find chiefly in exceptional people, not in ordinary folk such as ourselves. That there is an impulse to self-serving behaviour in us is clear enough, but it is not the full story. Alongside the greed and thoughtlessness of which we are capable, there are our myriad acts of kindness and consideration for others, from carefully chosen gifts to courteous behaviour, such as safe driving habits, blood donations and keeping noise levels down. In a world where the greatest well-being cannot be achieved by our individual efforts, it is surely clear that unless there is plenty of giving to and by others, such well-being will not last. This is partly why I give pride of place to the value of generosity, along with the truthfulness and integrity that it requires.

What are the evils that stand directly opposed to generosity? The ugly qualities that come to mind are selfishness, meanness, harshness, hardness of heart, indifference, callousness, greed, exploitation, theft, violence and at the worst end of this gang of evils, hatred – above all, hatred leading to murder.

Why do these terrible characteristics disfigure our world and at times our own lives? We need to put far greater effort into understanding the nightmare side of our natures and cultures. Is it the result of too much reptilian brain in us, our drive for self-preservation and self-assertion gone wildly amok? Is it what happens when the rich and powerful trample on the rest of us? Or is evil, as I once heard the eminent German theologian Jürgen Moltmann say, frustrated love of God? By this, he meant the perversion that happens when our vast capacity for total dedication fixes upon anything unworthy of it. Whatever the truth, at the very least, let us be keenly aware of everything that lovelessly opposes generosity of life in ourselves, in others and in our societies.

Integrity

We have already seen that a caring heart must go hand in hand with a caring mind, lest it be short-sighted and ineffective. The phrase 'hand in hand' is very revealing here because it takes us directly to the vital moral quality of integrity. My audiences often ask what this word means. I explain that it stands for wholeness and the absence of contradiction. It is present in us when word and action come together, when what we say and what we are and do are in harmony with each other in the service of truth and goodness. This latter qualification is important because it is possible for word and action to be at one in the pursuit of evil or selfish gains, as we saw in the life of Adolf Hilter. We would not therefore think of him as a person of integrity in the same way that we think of Mahatma Gandhi or Nelson Mandela.

Truthfulness

Truthfulness is the living heart of moral integrity. It is important to be quite clear here. I see truthfulness or honesty first and foremost as a love of and passion for truth, for facts, for understanding, for knowledge. It is the desire to be aware of what is going on, to be as free as possible of delusion, prejudice and error. In the second place, it is a commitment to speaking truthfully, with one vital qualification concerning situations where speaking the truth (as distinct from knowing it) endangers the freedom, and especially the lives of the innocent and vulnerable.

My own view of this contentious issue is that while it is always our moral duty to be truthful in the sense of wanting to know the truth, a quality supremely present in Gandhi, for whom God was truth and truth was God, there are some rare situations where a higher moral duty takes over – the duty to protect the innocent and vulnerable. What decent person would not lie to save the lives of his or her children, partner and friends or save them from harm?

Much less persuasive is the argument that it can be ethical to tell untruths in order to spare somebody's feelings – what we usually call 'white lies'. Most of us know exactly what is involved here because most of us have told such lies. It may seem like a concern for somebody's well-being; it may seem like generosity, sparing somebody a painful confrontation with facts about them. But are white lies really beneficial, at least when told to a mature, stable person rather than to a fearful child, or emotionally shattered adult? Or is it the easy option for the person who tells the white lie, preferring to gloss over something that will be hard to say and hard to hear? Does this not run the risk of preventing corrective action taking place? We all know from medical treatment that accurate diagnosis – in ordinary English, establishing the truth about our condition – is absolutely vital to healing, so there cannot be much debate about the essential link between truth and well-being. But in our dealings with others (apart from children or adults who are clearly vulnerable and in need of protection from hurt), isn't the really caring policy to have the courage to speak the truth, finding kind and sensitive ways of doing so? Don't we violate the principle of equality if we fail to do so, telling ourselves that we know best what is good for the person concerned?

Returning now to truthfulness, I want to point to some related values and qualities. To be honest and generous is also to be trustworthy and reliable, because people of integrity keep their word and show concern for the good of others. To value truth also means valuing self-knowledge, which is another reason for my doubts about the acceptability of white lies. Being honest with and about oneself, warts and all, must surely lead all of us to a keen awareness of our own weaknesses, wrongs and fallibility, unless it is very superficial indeed. In this case, we should be willing to hear things about ourselves that may be hard to bear. Thus a genuine love of truth must make us both open-minded and willing to learn from others, and also humble and realistic enough to acknowledge our limitations and failures. It should also make us judiciously critical about the things we hear from others, for they too are fallible and capable of deception, and truth is not well served by being gullible and naive.

There is a long-standing view in Western philosophy that knowledge can be defined as justified, true belief. It goes back to Plato, who was concerned to pinpoint the difference between reliable beliefs and unreliable ones (such as mere opinion) with knowledge seen as the most reliable precisely because genuine knowledge can be shown by facts and logic to be true. In short, it can be justified by reliable methods, unlike most of our opinions. For example, we can go out and check for ourselves, which means taking personal responsibility. We can check the credentials of those, like our experimental scientists, who say they have verified things, or accept their integrity until there is proof to the contrary, which shows respect. Plato's view is extremely important for ethics because knowledge in this sense cannot be had without honouring some key values such as reliability, responsibility and respect.

What about the evils that stand opposed to the attractive qualities of truthfulness and integrity we have been noting? I would say that the opposite of integrity is hypocrisy, saying one thing and doing another, pretending to a goodness we do not live out or even try to live out. Falsehood is another contrary quality, involving deceit and lies, or even only half-truths and the intention to mislead. And if an open, questing mind is essential if truth is to prevail, then closed, dogmatic and bigoted minds are also unethical, though not always so seriously as to qualify as outright evils, a word we generally reserve for the worst wrongs.

When integrity, truthfulness and knowledge are enriched by experience, by practical sense and a concern for the good of others, the result is the fine quality that we call wisdom. It is a great pity that so little is heard of it these days, when we are so obsessed with important but lesser goods, such as information. Without wisdom and the discernments and capacity for sound advice to which it gives rise, our quest for the greatest well-being is not likely to succeed, for the opposite of wisdom is foolishness, and foolishness is usually the prelude to trouble.

Respect
As a general rule, generosity means having respect for the basic humanity of all. This principle rests on the equal status of all people because of their ability to choose good over evil, right over wrong. It also rests on

a deep understanding that every human being needs to be recognised and affirmed as a uniquely valuable person whose potential for good matters greatly and whose failings and errors can so often be transformed and healed. Few things hurt or offend us more than to be treated with scorn, disdain or contempt, as if we don't matter. Being treated like this cuts our sense of self-worth, our dignity, to the quick. There is thus no question about the centrality of respect in the realm of conscience and thus in our prospects for flourishing.

But true respect calls for more than just words and politeness. If it is deep, it will involve a desire to understand others, and to benefit from the richness of their experience and from their capacity for generous, caring behaviour. In a world of many cultures, this also has to mean learning about other cultures in a spirit of sensitivity and openness to all goodness everywhere. Nothing less will suffice if we are to build a sustainable, enriching global future.

Do we owe respect to notorious evildoers such as Stalin, Hitler and Saddam Hussein, or to ordinary people convicted of viciously cruel crimes? Here we need to think carefully. Commitment to the principle of concern for the common good means fostering care, concern, compassion and kindness. Tyrants such as the trio mentioned above did the exact opposite on a massive scale. Conscience itself therefore obliges us to condemn, and where necessary and possible, punish such wickedness. But at the same time, we must also not lose sight of three other ethical considerations. First, nobody is utterly and totally wicked, not even the worst evildoer, since even in such a person, there is a spark of goodness that needs to be acknowledged and respected – perhaps a love of animals or family. Second, where possible, every effort must be made to encourage such people to change their lives. This is obviously not feasible with Stalin and Hitler, but it can be resolutely tried with others such as the criminals I mentioned above. Such attempts will not have a ghost of a chance of working if we show these people disgust and contempt, rather than respect for their basic humanity, which does not mean condoning what they did. Third, we demean ourselves if we treat others who have done very bad things with contempt or cruelty.

Let me illustrate this consideration. Despots and dictators come in various forms. They can be found lording it over families, businesses, sports teams and even religious organisations, and they have a particularly nasty habit of turning up in politics. No morally concerned person or true democrat would ever defend these autocrats, or fail to applaud their downfall. For this reason, a few years ago, I rejoiced along with many others at the news that Saddam Hussein had been captured. Half an hour after hearing the news, I saw the images of a dishevelled and seemingly disorientated Hussein that were beamed to televisions around the world.

But the sight of 'the Butcher of Baghdad' having his mouth and teeth probed for all the world to see, the way one might check the mouth of a horse or dog, filled me with dismay – at all who were party to this assault on the dignity of his person. Every subsequent appearance of those images has caused me to have the same reaction.

This in turn has led me to reflect critically on my reaction. Was it a justified dismay, or was it misplaced concern? Have I gone soft on the type of grotesque bully that deserves the outright condemnation of all decent citizens? Or was my reaction the result of a commitment to decency and dignity, and not a denial of them?

The basic human equality of all people surely means that people committed to doing the right and honourable thing are bound to respect the dignity of all people, everywhere – including whatever holding cell Saddam Hussein was in when somebody authorised his check-up to be televised and shown to the world, just as it includes all people held captive anywhere, especially those in Iraq, or elsewhere at this time.

Mindful of the atrocities to which dictators like Saddam Hussein are so callously prone, many people will cry halt at this point and say that those who brutally and systematically strip others of their liberties, their rights and their lives, sometimes by means of torture, have forfeited their own dignity and deserve to be treated with contempt. They will say that Hussein falls into this category. They may even point out that the word dignity is defined by the *South African Concise Oxford Dictionary* (2002) as 'the state or quality of being worthy of honour or respect', adding that there is no way that Hussein could meet this definition. These people might say that by violating the dignity of others, he has forfeited all right to respectful treatment.

I am not one of these people. I favour the generous view of human dignity, not the harsh one. I do not believe that even the vilest of deeds renders any of us sub-human. I applaud the Taoist symbolism of yin-yang, in which a tiny bit of the lighter half of that famous symbol is present in the darker half, and vice versa, seeing in it a reminder that none of us is wholly good, and none totally and irredeemably evil.

There are both secular and religious grounds for this approach to human dignity. Both of them pick up the dictionary definition that links dignity to worth. Secularist philosophies trace the worth or value of human life (and sometimes also animal life) to its marvellous biological complexity and richness, its transience, its potential for beauty and goodness, its fragility and – perhaps especially – its uniqueness, every one of us being irreplaceably special and distinctive. Religious believers trace the value of life to its source in the loving intentions of a divine creator, and to the example of the great spiritual guides of history and their great messages of boundless mercy and compassion.

For secularist and believer alike, at least in Western cultures, there is a well-known Christmas image that says it all: the image of a newborn baby in an animal feeding trough on a winter's night long ago, watched over by shepherds and hailed by kings. Among the messages beamed out to the world by this image, there is one about the value and dignity of even a helpless infant from a poor, small-town family in a land ruled mercilessly by the despots of Imperial Rome and their local deputies. Is it stretching the profoundly generous message of this scene too far to believe that the ethics of love that entered world history that night extends to even the cruelest of despots, recognising even in them a spark of value and worth, so that to infringe their dignity debases the victor perhaps more than the victim?

Turning now to other aspects of the ethics of respect, I need to include self-respect in this discussion. This is not to be confused with arrogance, undue pride or vanity. What then is self-respect all about? Its basis is the equality of all people as individually unique human beings. Truthfulness means that I must acknowledge my own basic value and potential for good, and so must everybody else acknowledge theirs. When we do this, self-respect is present. This is not self-importance; it is realism about a very important truth. Low self-esteem, on the other hand, is a problem for the quest for maximum well-being because its tendency is to reduce our capacity for effort, which in turn means less ability to support others where needed, which, as we have repeatedly seen, is of the very essence of human goodness. Self-respect needs more than this first step of acknowledging our own uniqueness, value and potential for good. It needs the affirmation of others who are important to us: parents, other family members, teachers, friends, mentors, colleagues, superiors at work and, for many people, religious guides.

Cultural diversity has important implications for respect as we lay foundations for a global vision and practice of the good, the beautiful and the true, most of all in places where people of different cultures live side by side. Real respect for people from different cultures, as distinct from mere lip-service, means taking trouble to understand the basics of their culture. We will therefore explore ways of achieving this in Chapter Five. For now, it is enough to emphasise that there is no other way to show genuine regard for cultures other than our own than by making the effort to know something about their values, beliefs, customs, ways of greeting people, dress codes and the like. Just how much real respect do we show our fellow-citizens of the Islamic faith when we haven't much idea what Ramadan is all about, or if we think that they regard the Qur'an in the same way that Christians regard the Bible, or if we show scorn for their dress code?

The ethics of respect also include respect for people's property, by which I mean things that they validly own. None of us can thrive without a certain minimum of possessions: clothing, basic equipment for our work and for our cleanliness, somewhere secure to live, and so on. And we all have a right, I would argue, to own whatever we ourselves create. These and other ethically and honourably owned possessions must be respected as ours and we must all respect the same right for everybody else.

Things are different when it comes to ill-gotten possessions such as the fruits of plunder, violence, theft and exploitation. Here, the duty to show respect can lead to a duty to remove those possessions. Liberating slaves and confiscating child pornography are obvious examples, but what about those of us who get rich because we pay our workers as little as possible? I can see no general rules here apart from the principles of respect for the rightful property of others, including their skills and labour, and valuing those things accordingly and what they give us, so those situations have to be checked out carefully and accurately before right and wrong can be established.

Here again we see just how intimately generosity and truth are intertwined. In order to let a generous heart lead to deep respect and to appropriately caring action, we must know enough about people's situations, especially by listening to them, to find out what would be appropriate. We must form a sense of what inspires, moves, or at times debases them, and empathise with it, looking beyond anything that is wrong to what could be made right, and above all, developing a fine sense of the sometimes strange goodness of others. Then respect is truly deep; then it builds bonds between people who can otherwise so easily form suspicions, dislikes, resentments and hostilities.

Opposed to respect are such unwelcome, and at times, ugly behaviours, such as undue familiarity, discourtesy, impoliteness, scorn, insult, contempt, and of course, plain disrespect, as well as theft, as we saw in connection with respect for people's possessions. It is quite revealing that we should have a substantial vocabulary of terms for a lack of respect, perhaps showing that this is a widespread moral lapse and that we don't take it seriously enough, like those who examined the teeth of the captured Saddam Hussein under the gaze of television cameras for all the world to see.

Justice and fairness

In high school, I was once severely punished by a physically massive teacher who had lost his temper because of cheek from another boy. He then became red-faced with anger when he discovered that I had left a book at home that I needed. I certainly deserved a rebuke, but not the physical lashing he proceeded to administer. Today, what he did is a crime; in those days, it was commonplace. Anyway, I felt that his action was utterly unfair and humiliating. This was not a conclusion that I reached after a process of rational thought. It leapt instantly and powerfully to life right then at the sheer unfairness of the punishment in relation to the quite minor offence, and at the humiliation it involved. Now, over forty years later, my indignation is still strong when I think back to that day.

Another spontaneous reaction in me that day was to lose respect for a man I had until then admired and liked. Had he made some gesture of regret, even privately, that would have ended the matter, but he showed no sign ever of having made a bad mistake, a mistake involving the unfairness of humiliation and a punishment that was grossly too severe for my minor wrongdoing. He showed no recognition that his action was an act of cruelty and disrespect.

Why did I react as I did? Is a sense that things must be done fairly so deeply ingrained in all of us that most people would react much as I did? Looking back, I can see my reactions in a light that was not available to me then. I can see now that injustice damages us far more deeply than at a physical level, serious though that can be. It damages our sense of self-worth, our basic human dignity, and until corrected by some act of contrition by the person who acted unfairly, the sense of injury smoulders on, burns on in us, alienating us, perhaps permanently, from those who thus wronged us.

When we understand the principle of human equality, we can also see that it means treating people even-handedly and therefore fairly and justly. What is fair or just about discriminating against people because of differences such as language, skin colour, gender or belief? Are we not all entitled to fairness? Putting somebody at a disadvantage because of things they can't help is not only unjust; it is also cruel because it makes them suffer, which clearly violates the principle of generosity. Similarly, the practice of doing favours for one's political or religious associates in situations where even-handedness towards all is due also violates the need to act fairly.

Closely related to fairness is justice, a moral value with a great and noble history. Recall, for example, the magnificent words of Micah, the ancient Hebrew prophet of the eighth century BCE: 'What does the Lord require of you, but to do justly and love kindness, and walk humbly with your God' (Micah 6:8). In modern times, we have seen the rise and triumph of great movements for social justice and human rights, campaigning against evils such as slavery, racism, the oppression of women, and the curse of poverty. Nobody with a caring heart can be indifferent to the cruelty and utter unfairness of these evils, or any other evils where people are treated as second or third best because of things they cannot change, which includes skin colour, gender and sexual orientation.

In his famous book *Situation Ethics*, Joseph Fletcher wrote that 'justice is love distributed' (1966: 87). I think that this is an important insight, enabling me to believe that fairness and justice are generosity distributed in a spirit of even-handedness to all. This lets us see justice as a moral value of utmost importance, and that its opposite of injustice involves the related evils of discrimination, cruelty and disrespect. Small wonder that many of us believe that there can never be peace until there is justice.

To my mind, an especially terrible form of injustice happens when one religion or philosophy is given superior legal status over others in the same society, even if its members form a majority. It is, I believe, deeply wrong to discriminate against somebody for what their souls, their innermost, deepest beings, hold sacred. We had this evil in South Africa during apartheid, when members of a conservative version of Protestant Christianity gave their religion status and privileges such as access to schools and public broadcasting that were denied to others, such as the country's Muslim, Hindu and African traditionalist people.

Happily, the campaign that some of us waged against such unfairness was successful. The new South Africa has a constitution that guarantees freedom and equality of status to all belief-systems. There were those who argued for a Christian state because most South Africans define themselves as Christians of one kind or another. My own answer was that catering merely for the majority is only acceptable when it is clearly impossible to cater for all alike, which was certainly possible in this instance. Adopting a bill of rights that treats all faiths and all non-religious belief-systems even-handedly and favours none ensures that there is equality for them all. This is what South Africa did in its 1996 constitution, which means justice for everybody, and not only for a majority.

Here too, there is a crucial challenge facing the USA today because of the great growth in the political influence of extremely conservative Christians. The continued separation of church and state – indeed of all belief-systems and the state – is absolutely vital if there is to be freedom and justice for all. Blurring this separation is bad for politicians because it denies them the independent, critical, prophetic voices they must have, lest power break free of conscience, and it is especially bad for religion because it weakens, rather than enhances, its spiritual and moral influence. This is an issue where the South African experience could be of great value to the USA because we have lived under a dispensation where an important section of Christianity lost its soul through too close a link with the state.

Inclusiveness

It should now be clear why inclusiveness is so important. It means, as we have seen, wanting what is good for all. It means that a parent who neglects one of his or her children, a society that neglects an ethnic minority, an approach to conscience that ignores three quarters of the world's moral wisdom, and a world where one fifth of humanity lives in dire poverty, are all guilty of failing to enlarge their active concern to include everybody in principle, and in practice anybody that we affect.

One of my favourite ethical maxims is said to have been coined by William Temple, the Anglican Archbishop of Canterbury when the Second World War broke out, though I have not been able to verify the source. It goes like this: 'Moral progress means enlarging the circle of your concern'. The implication is that we will not have progressed enough until that circle includes everybody and everything that can suffer harm. This does not only mean all people, it also means nature. In a relational world, people are part of nature even though human consciousness, conscience and complex languages may set us apart from other living things. If the opposite of concern for the well-being of others is harm and destruction, then anything that can suffer harm qualifies to be inside that circle of concern, as today's environmental movement so clearly recognises.

This means more than caring for nature because we depend on it; it means caring for nature in its own right. Nor should we limit the environment entirely to things green, for there is also the built or brown environment. Buildings and bridges don't suffer pain, but they can certainly be damaged and destroyed. Except when this is done correctly in a process of beneficial improvement, damage and destruction of this kind spell loss, and at times, suffering to people, so it is important to include respect for the built environment in our concern for inclusiveness – a point with implications for a concern for beauty, which we will explore a bit later in this chapter and the next.

If considerate, generous and truthful living requires that our care and concern must extend to as many others as practically possible, then it is clearly wrong to exclude anybody, or to treat them as inferior in any way as this is the opposite of inclusiveness. Once again, the South African experience of apartheid is powerfully relevant, but it is by no means the only one. Black Australians, US citizens, and Britons enjoy equality before the law, but still sometimes experience racist attitudes and treatments, while Europe's Jews and other minorities suffered the genocidal savagery of the Nazis within living memory. The emergence of the term 'ethnic cleansing' and the recent horrors of the Balkans, Rwanda, Palestine and Israel, and more recently, the Sudan, show us only too painfully just how far the world is from a culture of inclusion.

Responsible, caring effort

When I talk about responsible, caring, and hence moral effort, I mean making things better, even in small ways. When I was writing this book, I sent a short portrait of moral goodness to my local newspaper, *The Witness*, inviting readers to let me have their views of the same subject. One person felt I was putting too much emphasis on active concern, and mentioned the goodness of elderly people who bravely and positively endure difficult circumstances, but without much activity, in the sense of sustained, energetic work for others. Having recently had personal experience of such people, I certainly agreed. One of them, a much-loved godmother, was very elderly, bedridden and fading. But she never failed to be cheerful and kindly when her family and friends came to her bedside. To my mind, she was definitely making an effort to keep on top of her situation in a brave and caring way. Compared to the busy, energetic nurses and other caregivers who looked after her, we might think that she was inactive. But in a way suited to her situation, she was in fact anything but inactive. I think she was making a great effort at being the best kind of person she could in her situation, and she succeeded brilliantly until her dying day.

A sustainable, thriving world of fulfilled people living in a healthy environment will not come about because we all feel deeply committed to it, important though commitment is. It will only come about if we *do* something to make it happen. This is why I have emphasised *active* concern in my approach to a life inspired by conscience. Effort or action driven by a caring heart is therefore another core value. Even what seem to be very small or minor ways of acting, such as taking a real interest in the people who visit you when you are bedridden and infirm, or holding their hands tightly and lovingly, can have great moral effect. These things touch us and inspire us, leading to greater and more kindly efforts from us, which ripple out to others and benefit them.

This is one of the most wonderful things about moral effort: how it grows as it flows, picking up energy and commitment from the waiting goodness in all of us. Unlike money in our pockets, the more moral effort we expend, the more we have to give.

When the young and unknown M.K. Gandhi was thrown off a train at Pietermaritzburg station in South Africa in the winter of 1893 because of his colour, his reaction was initially only a resolve in his own mind: to seek a better way forward. Sharing this with others allowed its inherent goodness to flow and grow, so that it became a movement in South Africa, and then in India, when he returned there in 1914. Back in his homeland, its growth really took off, leading in 1947 to India's liberation from colonial rule. In the USA, Gandhi's path of non-violent resistance inspired Martin Luther King Jr.'s work for civil rights for African Americans, bringing great goodness there too. This is why I want to keep emphasising the importance of adding whatever effort and action our situations permit, however seemingly minor, to the things conscience calls on us to care about, because there is such stunning proof that even very small beginnings such as a noble resolve in somebody's mind can change the world, *so long as it passes from our minds to our lips, to our hands and our feet, even if in small ways, and thus to others.* Gandhi's story is proof that in the world of conscience, small can be very big indeed (for Gandhi's story, see Brown and Prozesky 1996; Chadha 1998: 52ff.).

I use the word 'resolve' in the previous paragraph because it plays a key part in moral effort. What ends up as something we do to bring about benefit, using our energy, our strength and our talents, often begins deep inside us as inner strength – as moral backbone. Notice what this metaphor means. It means taking responsibility for things and not sitting back waiting for others to do something. It means strength of purpose and perseverance rather than half-heartedness, initiative rather than passivity, self-discipline and self-control, rather than weakness of will.

Moral backbone sometimes requires courage when things get tough or dangerous, and sometimes it requires sacrifices. There is plenty of evil and danger around, which often brings power and wealth to those who cause or connive at it. They are not going to give it up lightly; on the contrary, they will fight for it. Good people will not defeat evil, if they flinch or flee when sacrifices have to be made, especially the sacrifice of their own safety and security. Good people have to take responsibility for the work that must be done, if we are going to succeed in building a better, happier world.

Most of all, the quest for a better local and global future needs all the energy we can give, ranging from the cheerful courage and prayers of a dying loved one to the vigorous generosity of the healthy and well resourced. Small wonder that most good and decent people see laziness as an important moral failing, or that the Book of Proverbs in the Bible should counsel the sluggard to consider the busy ways of the ant and be wise (6:6).

What are the evils that oppose and undermine moral effort? Laziness, indifference and lip-service all involve lack of effort, as does the 'free-rider' – the person who cleverly benefits from the work of others, without making a contribution themselves. But there is also effort, even fanatical effort, of a harmful, destructive kind, which is obviously damaging to the cause of the good. Hitler's Germany was very hard-working, but in wickedly murderous ways, so effort alone is not part of a healthy set of moral values. It must be effort that assists, benefits and promotes the well-being of those it affects.

Freedom

Few human passions are as strong these days as the passion for liberty. Perhaps it is what prompted the great nineteenth-century German philosopher Hegel, in a rare moment of clarity, to declare, as quoted by Peter Singer in his 'Past Masters' book *Hegel*, that 'the history of the world is none other than the progress of the consciousness of freedom' (1983: 11). Although words such as 'liberty' and 'freedom' have become modern mantras, words of great power and unquestioned good, we still need to reflect on them, widening and deepening our understanding of freedom from its important, but limited, social and political meaning.

To do this, I want to suggest two things: that we think of genuine freedom as release from the captivities that frustrate our quest for the greatest well-being and from all damage to our sense of self-worth, and secondly that we misunderstand it until we see it, first and foremost, as an ethical and spiritual reality.

The link with spirituality is reflected in the source of the word 'spirit'. Coming from terms meaning the breath and the wind, it points to a deep, often mysterious dimension of our being – our true and living selves where, if we wish to be whole beings, we encounter and embrace life's deepest sense of worth and meaning, experiencing it as more real and important than anything else. Religious people speak of this encounter as the sacred or the divine, but as these are not universally accepted terms, the policy of even-handed inclusiveness bids me to prefer other words for it, such as the description given in the previous sentence.

My own experience of this reality is that it brings about a sense of joyous, wordless freedom, of existing in a space of supreme beauty and generosity that invites me to exult in the opportunity to be the truest and most generous person I can be, no matter how often I may fail, given the realities of my time, place and make-up. It feels like being free of the downward pull of habit, cultural demands, dogmas, fears, traditional expectations and peer pressure to be something other than the unique best that I can be. It comes with the realisation that although my body can be locked away, there is a dimension of my being that only

I can lock and unlock, where all of us become either our own jailers, or our own liberators.

This understanding came home to me towards the end of apartheid in South Africa, during an experience of political arrest and physical captivity that mercifully proved very short-lived. While it lasted, it was certainly very frightening, and none of us knew at the time that it would be short-lived. The apartheid police had violently invaded one of the campuses of my university, prompting a group of about two hundred staff and students on the Pietermaritzburg campus to march in protest. The moment we left the university grounds for a public street, we were stopped by a large company of heavily armed police, arrested, loaded into their lock-up vehicles, and taken off into custody.

People had died in such situations, so it was definitely no picnic. I remember vividly the fear that I felt, and the icy anxiety of not knowing where or how it would end, for there were no democratic guarantees or respect for human rights in those days. But what I remember most is my own sense that although my body was under the total control of violent men serving an evil regime, a deeper part of me was as free as the wind, the part of me that knew I had a choice about how I would handle myself in that situation.

Would I let hatred of those captors and their masters take over or not? Would I face and control my fear or give in to it? Would I be calm and confident or not? And so, sitting there against a wall on a cold, concrete floor, side by side with colleagues and students, and very much a captive, I felt a moment of exultant liberty at the sense that my spirit was mine and nobody else's; that in a way I still cannot explain adequately, reality, whether divine or natural, is such as to give us – *give* us, notice – this deepest of experiences of who and what we can be: either part of the system of cruelty, violence and lies, or part of their transformation by means of generosity, care and truth.

This is what I mean when I say that freedom is essentially a spiritual and ethical reality, which also lets us see why freedom cannot be an unqualified good. Freedom is good only to the extent that it lets us be good and do good. Hitler and Stalin wielded virtually total power over their domains, probably more free of external control than anybody else in history, but theirs was an unspeakably evil freedom, like the 'freedom' of the slave-owner to do as he pleased with his slaves, or the 'freedom' of the child rapist, and on a massive scale affecting many millions of lives. Freedom in its essence is not an evil, but it can be wantonly used for evil.

Emphasising inner freedom as I have in no way lessens the importance of other kinds of liberty, or the evil of other kinds of captivity. It is good for us to be free of fear and bodily harm, to be free of domination, to have freedom of speech, association, belief and movement. But anybody who has had personal experience of a liberation struggle for those freedoms will know that these struggles are fuelled by a very deep and powerful passion. This is rooted in the feeling of resistance, and at times outrage, that comes from being wrongly held back from self-realisation. For example, in the struggle for gender equality, knowing that you, as a woman, are fully capable of doing what the male controllers of your society say you cannot and may not do, such as being a priest, or that you as a free thinker are being denied equal status and expression by a bigoted political community.

It should now also be clear why democratic societies attach so much importance to autonomy – perhaps even too much. Meaning the ability to govern ourselves, autonomy is widely seen as a basic human right. I think that this is correct, for the power to rule ourselves is exactly what I was referring to above in the account of my arrest experience.

What happened to me was an experience of the reality and depth of our right of self-rule as a sacred space within each of us. Brutal captors can terrify us into subservience of body and words by beating us, or even just threatening to do so, but they can never *make* us respect them, let alone love them, as distinct from getting us to pretend to do so, lest they beat us again. Over those supreme values, we are truly sovereign, and this, I believe, is the basis of the passion for autonomy. However, what we must also always remember is that we are part of a relational world that sets real limits to how we can use our power and our right to rule ourselves – as we saw in the previous chapter.

So we find that conscience requires commitment to the greatest freedom that is consistent with humane, truth-loving values, and it requires a special sensitivity to and respect for the inner freedom that I have been emphasising. Parents, educators and religious leaders have a particularly important function in cherishing and encouraging it in all who look to them for guidance, resisting absolutely the temptation to play God over other people's spirits.

During a sabbatical in Oxford in the spring of 2004 when I was researching aspects of this book, I found a most wonderful illustration of the inner freedom I have been emphasising. I want to invite readers to join me as I relive that experience, coming with me in their imaginations, walking along Parks Road away from Broad Street in central Oxford, to Keble College for a visit to its imposing red-brick chapel. This alone is well worth visiting, but the richest experience takes place in a small side-chapel. There you will find the original of Holman Hunt's famous painting 'The Light of the World', inspired by the following words from Revelation in the New Testament: 'Behold, I stand at the door and knock. If any man hears my voice and opens the door, I will come in and sup with him and he with me' (3:20).

I had seen small reproductions of the painting before, with its striking depiction of Christ holding a lantern at his left side and knocking at the door of the soul with his right hand. The original, superbly lit, is something else altogether, a work of great beauty and symbolic power to which I can do no justice in words. What I can say is that for me, the most powerful feature of the painting is Hunt's depiction of the door of the soul, for it has no outside handle and can thus only be opened from within.

The message of this symbolism is that there is a space in all of us where we alone are sovereign, a space made sacred by that sovereignty, and especially by the ultimate respect it receives even from a deity, who is seen as waiting to be invited into the soul, and not as invading it.

This is exactly what I have tried to emphasise in the view of freedom just given, and indeed in the emphasis I have placed in the experience of deep value earlier in this chapter.

As for the evils that oppose true and responsible freedom, they range from such obvious examples as physical control of people who are not criminals, to the subtle denials of liberty that take the form of mental and financial domination. Anything that denies or lessens human creativity must also be seen as wrong, particularly when the victims are children.

Beauty

In some of the ancient ethical and religious wisdom of the world, there is a wonderful emphasis on the union of the good, the beautiful and the true. In Western cultures and perhaps some others, by contrast, conscience has often been taken to be about goodness and truth, but not so much about beauty. We even have a separate discipline to study it, called aesthetics. This is a pity because who of us can deny that beauty has very great value for us, or that we make an ethical judgement when we say that certain behaviours are lovely or ugly? So I want to include beauty in my list of core values. But in doing so, it is essential to explain that beauty in the domain of conscience does not cover all kinds of beauty, only those for which we can be held responsible. This excludes having a gorgeous face or figure, but it includes the kind of bodily presence we manifest and the care we take of our appearance and our space.

Somebody who takes trouble to put flowers in his or her home or workplace is doing this by choice and enriches those who see the flowers. I would call this an ethical action because of the generosity it involves in bringing happiness to others. The same applies to town planners, architects and others who have the power to make our surroundings as pleasing to live in as possible. It also applies to beauty of sound. A love of music in its many forms is common to people of all cultures, and who can deny the good it does, making us feel happy, inspired, comforted, or relaxed? I think that this also applies very much to education, for a place of learning that is attractive and educators that are generous are more effective than ones that are drab or dull.

During the experience of arrest and short-lived captivity that I described earlier, we were later moved to and locked up in the holding cells that were normally used for prisoners awaiting trial, before being ushered into a midnight courtroom, warned to appear at a later date, and allowed to go home after the head of the university had stood bail for us. Even under apartheid, for all its evils, people awaiting trial were presumed to be innocent until found guilty by a court of law. Yet my abiding memory of the cell I was in is just how revoltingly ugly it was: bleak, forbidding and thick with the stench of fear and urine.

A forest after a bad fire caused by a lightning strike is a dismayingly ugly sight, but it is not morally ugly. Those cells were avoidably ugly, so their ugliness is a moral offence. Not even a criminal convicted of wicked crimes should be subjected to such disgusting places. The memory of it makes me wonder at criminology and criminal procedures. I do not expect prisons to look like luxury holiday resorts, but why do they have to look so depressing most of the time? To my mind, such ugliness will undermine efforts to rehabilitate the inmates for a worthwhile life when they have served their terms, such is the effect of context on us.

So it seems to me to be exactly right, returning now from ugliness to beauty, that places where goodness is taken seriously should also be made as beautiful as possible. If a university must choose between an attractively gardened campus and a good library, it must favour the library. But I see no excuse, when funds are not so tight, for any failure to ensure that our places of learning are pleasing to the eye and the senses, and at the very least, tidy, clean and free of litter. And I feel only gratitude for places of worship in all the faiths I have encountered where beauty is taken seriously. My own preference runs to gothic architecture, candles and stained glass windows, but I have also been uplifted by the sparer kind of graceful design that we find in other approaches to beauty, as in some of the mosques I have visited.

To round off my discussion of the core moral values that all of us need to know, understand, and of course, practise, here they are for ease of reference, together with some of their related values:

Beneficence values	*Integrity values*
Generosity	Truthfulness, which involves:
Respect	Reliability
Fairness	Trustworthiness
Inclusiveness	Self-knowledge
Moral effort	Open-mindedness
Freedom	Judicious criticality
Beauty	Wisdom

THE WORLD'S GREAT STREAMS OF CONSCIENCE

The core values presented above come from my understanding of human nature and the drive for the greatest well-being to which it gives rise, embedded in our relational world. This method, with its heavy reliance on similarities of personal experience across cultures, raises an important question: what about the values taught by the great spiritual and ethical traditions of the world? For it is these, rather than reflections on human nature, that shape most people's sense of right and wrong.

In order to link my set of values with these great traditions and to show their members the respect they deserve, I believe that a basic knowledge of these traditions is needed if we are to advance towards a genuinely inclusive global ethic. We need to know at least the main landmarks on the map of the world's moralities – of *orbis moralis* – the world as home to conscience, as we might call it. In academic circles, this is known as comparative ethics (De Gruchy and Prozesky 1991).

Twelve great value-systems

In the world today, there are probably as many different value-systems as there are distinct cultures, making a detailed knowledge of them an impossibly huge task. For the purposes of this book, something much less ambitious must suffice, namely a knowledge of the world's most widely held ethical traditions, which for both accuracy and convenience, I reckon to be twelve in number. They are the following, roughly in chronological and regional order:

- Indigenous or ethnic moralities
- The ethics of Judaism
- Christian morality
- Islamic morality
- Hindu ethics
- Buddhist ethics
- Confucian ethics
- Taoist ethics
- Western philosophical ethics
- Secular moralities
- Feminist ethics
- The global ethics movement

Giving people the respect that is their due means knowing what has shaped them and what motivates them ethically. Most people have formed their moral sense from one of these traditions and approaches, but in today's world of increasing, side-by-side cultural diversity, we and the people we work and live with will also be influenced to some extent by one or more of the others.

I find that this policy gains depth and insight when it includes a basic grasp of the history that has produced the various moral systems. This is also a long, complex and very rich story, so we need a way of simplifying it without distortion. The most helpful way of doing this, to my mind, is to use and slightly extend the proposal by New Zealand's seminal religious and ethical thinker, Lloyd Geering, in his booklet *Creating the New Ethic* (1991: 7ff.). I will outline his theory and then add my extension to it.

Conscience in indigenous ethnic cultures

The first part of the theory is that for many thousands of years, the human presence on this planet took the form of countless local cultures that had no contact with each other, except for a few neighbours. These cultures were based on things such as a shared language, territory and sense of kinship. Geering has proposed that we call them 'ethnic moralities' (1991: 7) because of these shared characteristics. Sometimes the same sort of thing is called indigenous, so I have used both terms in my list. The moral cultures of the Aborigines in Australia, Native Americans, traditional African societies, the ancient Israelites, Japan's Shinto tradition and New Zealand's Maori people are examples. In these cultures, religious beliefs are fused with moral values to form a single whole. Today's Western-derived distinction between sacred and secular was evidently quite unknown in these cultures and their surviving examples.

Trans-ethnic moralities

Approximately two thousand five hundred years ago, over a relatively short period, a series of very far-reaching religious, philosophical and ethical changes took place across Asia and into ancient Greece, which radically changed the world map of conscience. So profoundly have they transformed the heart and soul of much of the world that the twentieth-century German philosopher Karl Jaspers saw the period of their emergence as the most important turning point in world history. He therefore named it the Axial Age, from the word 'axis', meaning a pivot or axle. At this time, a series of highly influential moral and spiritual teachers appeared, quite independently of one another, calling for an ethical and spiritual sense far larger in scope than individual ethnic communities (Geering 1980: 66ff.).

In China, there was Confucius and Lao Tzu, legendary founder of the Taoist tradition whose famous yin-yang symbol is now known worldwide. In India, the Buddha and the Mahavira, founder of the Jain tradition (with an ethic of non-injury that strongly influenced Gandhi) appeared, launching the great movements associated with them and continuing their messages to this day. In ancient Persia, we find the Prophet Zoroaster, and in ancient Israel, the great Hebrew prophets Jeremiah, Isaiah and Ezekiel, to mention only three. Not long afterwards, the first philosophical ethics of the Western tradition appeared in Greece in the work of thinkers such as Socrates, Plato and Aristotle.

These Axial Age teachers and thinkers were followed, centuries later, by what are arguably the two most ethically influential figures of all, Jesus of Nazareth and the Prophet Muhammed. In every case, we find the use of writing to express and spread the moral visions associated with these figures, something absent in many of the older, ethnic moralities.

The messages of these hugely influential figures led to the fairly rapid growth of major new movements, which were (and remain) for the most part both ethical and religious – the exception to this dual character being the ancient Greek moral philosophers. These new movements gradually won adherents from ethnic cultures far removed in kind and in place from those of their founding figures, often causing those older, ethnic moralities to merge completely with the newer movements and lose their once distinctive identity. For example, the ethical tradition of the ancient Egyptians has vanished in the wake of the advances first of Christianity, and then Islam. For this reason, Geering proposes that we call these highly expansive, newer ethical systems that go back to the Axial Period 'trans-ethnic moralities' (1991: 7ff.).

The coming of a secular/global conscience

Geering sees a third phase or type of morality emerging during the past few centuries, initially in Western Europe and North America, but also now found in many other parts of the world such as Australia and New Zealand (1991: 7ff.). Here we find an emphasis on the needs of the present life, rather than an afterlife, and of the whole world, rather than particular traditions. It is shaped by human reason rather than faith, by scientific knowledge, secular Western philosophy, experiences of oppression and democratic ideals, and by the emergence (or perhaps re-emergence) of a belief that morality and religion as traditionally understood and practised are in fact distinct spheres and that some religious beliefs and practices are themselves in certain respects problematic – for example, when used to foster division, rather than unity, among the people of the world, or at times using persecution, rather than showing tolerance or mutual acceptance.

Given such a differentiation of ethics and religion, Geering proposes that we therefore think of this third major development in the story of ethics as 'secular/global morality' (1991: 7ff.). It is here that his proposal might perhaps be modified into two new forms or stages of ethics. One of them we can safely call secular because of its independence from (and at times hostility towards) religion, and its this-worldly focus. Marxist, secular humanist and some radical feminist approaches to good and evil, right and wrong, are the main examples. The second form that I see here is the quest for a global ethic. Having both religious and non-religious or secular strands, it might be a bit misleading to call it secular, which is why I see it as a distinct, new ethic, indeed as the most recent to emerge. As yet incomplete, it is nonetheless important enough to merit further discussion later in this chapter.

To the best of my knowledge, the first person to accept a real diversity of faiths and moralities in a single, embracing attitude, so laying the basis for a global ethic, was Mahatma Gandhi during his South African years. He, a Hindu influenced by Jainism, found friendships and support from Muslims, Christians and Jews in the already mixed populations of Durban and Johannesburg between 1893 and 1914. Steeped in the great Hindu text, the *Bhagavadgita*, he also loved the Sermon on the Mount and cared greatly for the Muslim minority of his homeland.

Just how powerful such a passion to include and embrace can be, was brought home to me during a visit to the Berlin Wall during my student days. At a bookstall near that ugly barrier between the communist east and the capitalist west, I found a brochure about the then divided city. It contained a quotation from Gandhi, saying that he wanted the winds of all cultures to blow freely in his face (Brown and Prozesky 1996: 21ff.). A world with many cultures must share that wish if we are to have peace and friendship rather than the bitterness and violence that we are seeing in the Middle East and elsewhere.

This historical overview leaves us with a picture of conscience starting in the distant past, long before written records, taking the form of the values of small-scale ethnic communities all over the world, many of which vanished as their members were drawn into the sweeping vision of those expansive trans-ethnic, axial movements, while others remain powerfully with us, as in Japan's Shinto and in Africa's traditional value-systems. Add to these the more recent rise of secular, feminist and global ethics and we have the twelve great value-systems in my list at the beginning of this section.

Convergence and divergence

What do we find when we journey into the world's most influential value-systems? What values do they teach, what do they forbid, and what motivation for a life of generosity and integrity do they give? In Chapter Three, we noted that our religions give different, and at times, incompatible reasons for ethical living, so we need not cover that ground again. What we must now note is some vital information about the main values they and secular moral systems teach.

When we explore these, we find agreement and disagreement, convergence and divergence, about what is right and wrong, good and evil, even within the same broad tradition, such as Islamic and Christian ethics. I want to give some examples of their divergence, and then emphasise their moral convergence because this is much more important for the great project of developing a globally shared conscience.

Imagine a conversation between three equally upright, devout and sincere individuals discussing whether it is ethical for a man to be married to more than one wife at the same time. One of them is Roman Catholic, the second is Muslim and the third is Zulu, who follows the traditional, ancestral wisdom of his people. The Catholic man declares polygamy to be morally wrong, quoting the Church in support of his view. The Muslim man cites the Qur'an and the Islamic tradition to disagree, saying that a man who can support them properly can have up to four wives at the same time. The Zulu man questions this limit, arguing that his culture permits a man to have many more wives if he can support them all. The trio is then joined by a radical feminist who faults the entire conversation and the traditions it reflects as deeply sexist and thus immoral. Why, she demands, is it a question about men? Why not also women? Why have there been hardly any cultures where women can have more than one husband as the same time, as in traditional, rural Tibet, if not because of a long history of male domination?

There was a time when most people dismissed those who valued the same behaviour or practice differently from themselves as very much in the wrong, or even as evil. I once heard a sincere Christian medical doctor dismiss African healing methods involving spirit mediums in strongly dismissive terms, in much the way all of us would condemn rape. But will this do for practices such as traditional healing, polygamy, the death penalty and abortion, about which people of broadly the same moral commitment and quality disagree? Of course not! On what *shared* moral grounds can I dismiss as immoral those decent, worried people who support the death penalty? Finding none, I conclude at least provisionally that we need a new category to handle this reality. I call it the reality of being *differently good*, while at the same time believing that there is a very real limit to what we can tolerate, lest we end up with the nightmare of moral relativism, according to which, there are no general rules about good and evil applying across cultures or even individuals.

If disagreements such as these were the most striking lesson of a journey into the heartlands of morality, we would be in trouble, especially where fundamentalists are a majority. They are people who see the world simplistically, but vehemently as a battle of good against evil, vilifying those whose value-systems contradict theirs. The good news is that these disagreements are not the dominant feature of the world's ethical experience, for it is a striking fact that, quite independently and despite grounding their moral teachings in very different understandings of the sources of good and evil, the great ethical traditions of the world have at their heart much the same basic moral message: *a repeated emphasis on the need for active concern for others, especially those who are vulnerable, coupled, conversely, with their warnings against selfishness, and harm to others and their possessions.* This, of course, is essentially the same basic moral principle as the one I have presented in this book as central to conscience, on the basis of our shared human nature.

What is the evidence from these traditions that gives rise to the claim that I have just made? The best thing for readers to do is make their own journeys of exploration and enrichment into these traditions. This can be done by reading about them and as a starting point, I provide suggestions in the bibliography at the end of this book. The most helpful short guide that I have found is in John Hick's book *An Interpretation of Religion*, because it summarises the relevant information from the faith-based traditions with great clarity and insight (1989: 299ff.).

But even more valuable for anybody living where there are people from several cultures close by is to make personal contact with informed members of other cultures and to hear from them about the values that they hold supreme. I have done this often over the years and found it to be a wonderfully enriching experience. Nothing clears ignorance and prejudice from our lives more effectively than a direct experience of the integrity and kindness of people from value-systems other than our own. Experiences of this kind have given me my main sense of the moral convergence of all the traditions that I have encountered, from Australian Aboriginal to Zen and Zulu. For the purposes of this book, however, I will use John Hick's material to illustrate the fact of convergence on the most important values, which I see as the great jewel of the world's collective ethical wisdom and a key part of the basis of a global ethic. This is the fact that they all emphasise the 'Golden Rule' in one or another of its formulations.

Readers of this book may be more familiar with or influenced by Christianity and its ethics than by any of the world's other value-systems, so I will begin there. If you ask a Christian what the supreme ethical principle is, the answer is almost always given by quoting two of Christ's most famous moral principles. The first is this: 'You shall love your neighbour as yourself' (Matthew 22:39), exactly echoing the much older commandment that we find in Judaism's Torah (the five books of Moses at the beginning of the Hebrew Bible), in the book of Leviticus (19:18). The other one is: 'Do to others what you would have them do to you' (Luke 6:31). The implication of the latter is that since we all want other people to treat us with respect, concern and honesty, that is how we must treat them, with the kind of genuine, active concern for their well-being that love requires.

In the ethics of Judaism, we find the original of the great principle of loving one's neighbour as oneself that Jesus of Nazareth quoted, and we also find the Talmud, an authoritative body of guidance about the Torah, saying that 'What is hateful to yourself do not do to your fellow man'. Islam's Hadith (traditions about the Prophet himself) cites Muhammed as saying that 'No man is a true believer unless he desires for his brother that which he desires for himself'. Hick also cites the same kind of central ethical principle from Hinduism, namely 'One should never do that to another which one regards as injurious to one's own self. This, in brief, is the rule of Righteousness'. From Buddhist ethics, we hear that 'As a mother cares for her son, all her days, so towards all living things a man's mind should be all-embracing'.

Ancient China produced two great trans-ethnic or axial movements, Taoism and Confucianism. The former contains the principle that the good person will regard the gains of another 'as if they were his own, and their losses the same way'. Confucius greatly emphasised the virtue of *jen* or humane behaviour, and laid down this principle: 'Do not to others what you would not like yourself'.

The same rule about concern for the good of others is taught in the value-systems of what Geering calls ethnic cultures. Certainly this is the case in those known to me. In traditional Zulu morality and others like it in South Africa, the central values are *ubuntu* (humanness) and *hlonipha*, meaning respect, illustrated by a proverb that tells us never to empty the cooking pot because we cannot know who might arrive hungry at our homes. What I have been told and read about Australian Aboriginal cultures reveals a similarly strong concern about the welfare of others in the community and of the land and all that lives and moves on it. During a walk to several traditional, sacred sites near Adelaide some years ago, the Aboriginal guide showed us a small ravine with a red ochre source, and very reverently painted some of it on his forehead, saying 'This is the blood of our Mother'. He also explained that the land itself was the sacred text, the Bible, of his culture, to be read by walking through it.

Western moral philosophy is a complex and mostly very abstract body of thought, but here too we find guidelines that are very similar to the Golden Rule or its clear implications. Over two centuries ago, the great German philosopher Immanuel Kant wrote that we must never use other people merely as means, but also always as ends in themselves, which is clearly an ethic of respect and concern for their valid interests. In the nineteenth-century, the English thinker John Stewart Mill gave highly influential shape to the view that the good and right way to behave is to do whatever will bring about the greatest happiness for the greatest number.

More recently we have seen the re-emergence in philosophical ethics of an emphasis on virtue, with special emphasis on values such as care and concern. Of particular interest in the ethics of care is the influence of women ethicists and of feminist ethics as a distinct and highly significant newer voice on ethical issues.

Another extremely important and revealing trend of the past few decades is practical or applied ethics. The work of Peter Singer is perhaps the most influential, with its deep concern with moral challenges such as extending our active concern to animals. Others are focusing their moral insights and passion on the environment, on the nature of justice, on poverty and violence. What does this mean if not a deep commitment to the cause of the common good, understood as care, respect and concern?

Turning now to the way secular humanists see morality, we need go no further than the words printed on the inside of each issue of *Free Inquiry*, the magazine of the USA's Council for Secular Humanism. Here we find a set of secular humanist affirmations and principles. They include the following: 'We believe in the common moral decencies: altruism, integrity, honesty, truthfulness, responsibility...' (*Free Inquiry*, 23(4), October/November 2003: 2). The match between these values and those of the others we have been reviewing is clear, a point made in an earlier issue of the same magazine dealing with the 'Humanist Manifesto 2000' (*Free Inquiry*, 19(4), Fall 1999: 4–20) where it is stated that the 'basic principles of moral conduct are common to virtually all civilisations – whether religious or not' (10).

The quest for a global ethic
The most recent trend is the quest for a global ethic, a set of core values ideally shared by all the world's people. In view of the emphasis in this book on maximum inclusiveness, readers will understand that I see this particular trend as the most significant of present-day developments in connection with conscience. Here the best-known person internationally is the radical German Catholic theologian, Hans Küng. In co-operation with others at the 1993 World Parliament of Religions in Chicago, he helped to produce a landmark statement of the values shared by the most widely followed faiths (Küng and Schmidt 1998). Although – so far as I am able to see – this approach leaves out some key voices such as those from traditional African and other ethnic cultures, some feminist voices and secular approaches to conscience, it remains a most important step towards the creation of a fully global set of values. For this reason, and because this book seeks to encourage the creation of a genuinely global ethic, I review it in greater detail than the value-systems reviewed above.

The 1993 Parliament of the World's Religions in Chicago took its inspiration from a first parliament of religions held a century earlier in the same city, and was attended by people from a great many faiths. It issued a document called 'The Declaration of a Global Ethic' (Küng and Kuschel 1993). The root idea of the Declaration is the important fact that we have already seen, namely the presence of a common set of core values in the teachings of the world's faiths and philosophies. The spiritual leaders who gathered in Chicago believe that this set of values can provide the basis for a global ethic. They see life on this planet as interdependent, so that we must all work together for a better world, and 'have respect for the community of living beings, for people, animals, and plants, and for the preservation of Earth, the air, water and soil'. They also believe very firmly that the Earth cannot be changed for the better until the consciousness of the individual is changed first.

The central principle of the Declaration is the Golden Rule: 'What you do not wish done to yourself, do not do to others. Or in positive terms: What you wish done to yourself, do to others!' This should be the irrevocable, unconditional norm for all areas of life, says the Declaration.

From this central principle, four other principles are drawn. All of them also appear in the teachings of most faiths. Firstly, there must be a culture of non-violence and respect for life, because all the religions teach the commandment, 'You shall not kill. Or in positive terms, have respect for life!' This also means that there must be no harm or injury, nor any bodily violation of any person.

Secondly, people must commit themselves to a culture of solidarity and to a just economic order. Noting that we live in 'a world in which totalitarian state socialism as well as unbridled capitalism have hollowed out and destroyed many ethical and spiritual values' and where greed has led to endless plunder, the Declaration points to yet another shared value in the various religions: 'Let there be no theft! Let people deal honestly and fairly with one another! Only so can the terrible poverty and suffering caused by exploitation be combatted, and human dignity protected'.

The third principle is that people must commit themselves to a culture of tolerance and a life of truthfulness. Around us there is a vast web of deception and distortion encouraged by ruthless politicians and profiteers, sometimes aided and abetted by educators, and even religious officials. Yet the ancient faiths all teach that 'You shall not lie! Or in positive terms: Speak and act truthfully!'

Commitment to a culture of equal rights and partnership between men and women is the fourth principle offered by the Declaration. All over the world, vast numbers of people still live in subjugation to others, notably children, women and minority groups. But the religions all teach that there must be no immorality between the sexes and that people must respect and love one another. I was particularly interested to see this principle being interpreted as forbidding gender exploitation and harm to those who are physically weakest, and not only as a condemnation of sexual licence.

Having set forth these principles of a global ethic, the Declaration ends with some stirring words: 'Together we can move mountains! Without willingness to take risks and a readiness to sacrifice there can be no fundamental change in our situation! Therefore we commit ourselves to a common global ethic, to better mutual understanding, as well as to socially-beneficial, peace-fostering, and Earth-friendly ways of life! We invite all men and women, whether religious or not, to do the same.'

A second approach to global ethics has been developed at the Institute for Global Ethics in the USA. Pioneered by its founding president, Rushworth M. Kidder, this approach uses conversations with ethically respected leaders from different cultures, in addition to surveys of the values rated most highly by people in a number of countries around the world. The result is striking and yet again provides strong support for the approach followed in this book. As described in his book *Shared Values for a Troubled World*, especially in the first and last chapters, Kidder has found that a set of eight moral values stands out as a shared core. They are: love, truthfulness, fairness, freedom, unity, tolerance, respect for life and responsibility (1994: 18). Bearing in mind that unity in this list is similar to what I have called inclusiveness, we can see how substantial the overlap is with the set of nine core values that I derived by my own method, before meeting Kidder and reading his book.

The very close fit between the moral principles of the 'Declaration of a Global Ethic', Kidder's results and my own ethic of inclusive well-being based on human nature and ordinary experience as set out in this book will be clear. Certainly the fit is close enough for my own ethic to have the support of core teachings in the world's most influential value-systems.

These agreements about basic values among the world's most influential moral teachings are the great lesson of convergence in the domain of conscience. Having arisen independently in each tradition, the basic principle of benefiting others and refraining from harm belongs to each, and none can presume to occupy higher moral ground than others, or see itself as a moral missionary charged with leading the rest out of darkness. Our separate histories, homelands and cultures have given the world a divided soul, but not, at heart, a divided conscience.

I think this means that we already have two strong foundations for a global ethic: human nature and the millennia of conviction and practice about core values built into today's great value-systems. The core principle of active concern for the common good, for maximum, inclusive well-being that they jointly teach provides an invaluable basis for negotiating the way to forge a truly inclusive global ethic and to handle the things about which we differ in a respectful way.

CONCLUDING SUMMARY
- Living in ways that promote the common good benefits from the greatly improved stock of relevant knowledge made available by the Information Age. This enhances our understanding of conscience

and its main values, and also our understanding of the world and its needs at a time when we must develop a truly inclusive global set of core values.

- Central to this improved understanding is the experience of deep ethical value, marked by generosity, cost, self-transcendence and rarity.
- Our desire for the greatest well-being gives rise to a lifestyle of care and concern involving a set of nine core values: generosity of spirit and action, truthfulness, integrity, respect, fairness, inclusiveness, responsible effort, freedom and beauty.
- Opposing them are the evils of hardness of heart, dishonesty, contempt for others, injustice, exclusion, laziness, control and domination over others, and preventable ugliness.
- The set of core moral values that derives from and expresses an ethic of care and concern aimed at enhancing the well-being of others as well as our own is essentially the same as the central moral teaching of the world's most influential ethical traditions, the subject matter of comparative ethics.
- For convenience and accuracy, these ethical traditions can be presented as a set of twelve, ranging from traditional, localised moralities such as those of Australia, the USA and Africa, to the ethics of the so-called world religions, to secular, philosophical and feminist ethical perspectives, and ultimately to today's movement for a global ethic.
- While there are important moral disagreements among these value-systems, there is also – more importantly – agreement about the heart of goodness, expressed typically in the various forms of the Golden Rule: do to others what you would have them do to you.
- Thus we have two powerful platforms for a truly inclusive global ethic: human nature itself and the collective independently developed moral wisdom of the world's ethical traditions past and present.

five

Making a Difference to Ourselves and Our Worlds

Hungry children who go barefoot to school, or shiver in the cold of a winter's morning in the world's sprawling shanty towns don't get food, shoes, heated classrooms and warm clothes because good, caring people feel bad about their suffering. If they get these benefits, it is because good, caring people *do something practical* to help. Becoming more generous, more committed to truth and integrity in our daily lives, and more conscious of the need to *work* for the greater well-being of all the world's people is the point and purpose of this book. Only generous *action* takes us to the places where sound values can make a real difference – in the world out there and in the inner world of our own personal commitment.

As I emphasised in Chapter One, democracy means that working for a global future where life will be better than it is now is the privilege and responsibility of *everybody* as moral equals. Cultural diversity means that people who are committed to the values that foster well-being need to understand, respect and embrace the moral wisdom of other cultures, particularly those present in their own workplaces, neighbourhoods and places of education. Globalisation means that we either create a humane planet, or wound it even more, perhaps irreparably. Avoidable suffering amidst fabulous wealth means that conscience can and must make a much bigger difference to the world than ever before.

How are we to go about deepening and strengthening our ability to make a better world? We can do this by understanding that ethical living is a matter of *managing life according to the principles of inclusive generosity and integrity* at all levels, from self-management to the wise and sustainable planetary management that is the greatest challenge of our times, especially for a global power such as the USA.

The foundation for managing our lives and world on the basis of humane values is, however, *personal* moral power, which is the subject of this chapter. In the previous chapters, we explored the ethical potential of the heart and mind. Now it is time to turn what we found there into a practical, holistic programme of personal moral growth. While the process can be done individually, it is better to share it, where possible, with somebody very close to us, such as a partner or trusted friend, someone who really cares about us, but is also aware of our shortcomings, and who is willing to help us to handle them in a sensitive and caring way.

FIVE COMMITMENTS

How, then, can we grow our consciences, our moral power? The practical guidance that follows is not aimed at pointing an accusing finger at evildoers and offering them a crash course in angelic goodness. Instead, it builds positively on the basic decency and moral potential in all people and offers a way to enrich and strengthen us ethically, covering the whole life-world of the individual. It has five commitments:

- to strengthen our own moral *character*;
- to ensure that our *contacts* with others – our relationships – foster their well-being;
- to make our *contexts* – such as family and workplace – as humanly rich and supportive as possible;
- to value *cultural diversity*; and
- to use whatever *controlling powers* we may have to foster strong ethical leadership.

This chapter is therefore about creatively managing character, contacts, context, cultures and our powers of control in ways that foster the greatest generosity and integrity, and in so doing, producing greater and more inclusive well-being. What follows sets the individual in a series of seven widening circles or contexts of living, from the most immediate to the most widely shared. These contexts are presented in step 4 below.

The emphasis on our contexts of living is extremely important, which is why I introduced it in Chapter One, and referred to it again and again in the other chapters. There is a widespread shortcoming in most of the approaches to both the ethical theory and practical ethics that I have encountered: too much emphasis on personal, individual moral strength – on things like character and virtue. These are essential aspects of the domain of conscience, but they are not enough. This is because we humans as individuals, for the most part, are simply not strong enough to enhance our moral fitness by sheer will-power, particularly in situations of great pressure to do otherwise. This is why there are so few ethical saints such as Francis of Assisi, the Buddha, Mother Theresa and Gandhi. The rest of us depend more or less heavily on supportive contexts to add power to our personal efforts and to protect us from the slide into selfishness, which comes all too easily.

So the basic formula for greater moral power (and hence well-being) is this: we need programmes of moral fitness and growth for both character and context, and thus for managing the relationships that come with each of our personal situations, each supporting and reinforcing the other.

TEN STEPS TO PERSONAL GROWTH

We turn now to a practical programme of personal moral growth. In the ten steps of the programme, the five commitments and the set of seven contexts mentioned above are explained. In setting them out, I have deliberately refrained from giving too much detail in the form of instructions or precise suggestions, opting instead for broader guidelines.

There is a very important reason for this policy: the broader, more general approach leaves much more scope for readers to be actively involved in working out the details for themselves – thereby giving plenty of space to their creativity. In ways that may seem very minor and informal, but which can be very powerful, all of us are capable of initiative, creativity and leadership, so it is essential that a programme of ethical growth should not rob people of the scope to use these abilities by being too much concerned with detailed instructions. Deepening and strengthening conscience – moral growth – is not like learning to use a sophisticated cell phone or digital camera, where exact instructions are essential. It is a blend of guidance and scope for moral creativity. What follows is designed to meet those two requirements.

Steps 1, 2, and 3 deal with a commitment to personal character building. Steps 4 and 5 deal with the commitment to develop contacts, contexts and cultures, marked by the values set out in the previous chapter, while steps 6, 7, and 8 return to personal character building. Step 9 is about the commitment to use our powers over others for inclusive benefit and with integrity, while step 10 completes the whole process on a high note of inclusive well-being. With these clarifications in mind, we can now go on to the ten steps towards enhanced, personal moral fitness, in which the things set out in the previous chapters are turned into a practical programme of self and contextual transformation.

Step 1: Understanding ourselves as unique centres of conscience

Every human being is a marvel of the cosmos or, for the religious, a marvel of creation. Scientists tell us that everything in the physical universe arose from the Big Bang some thirteen billion years ago. They tell us that the universe is fine-tuned for the emergence of a spectacular series of creative events leading to the arrival of the intelligent, creative species that is our own on this planet, with brains equipped for knowledge, value creation and moral choice. I sometimes invite my audiences to look at their hands, balling my fist, then opening it out in a gesture of peace and friendship, and then commenting on the power of the human hand to help or hurt. Then I invite them to look imaginatively beyond their hands to a magnificent ancestry going back to the spectacular origin of things in the Big Bang.

I find this a hugely inspiring, but also hugely humbling thought: that we humans and all things go back to this common birth of the energy and matter of life, yet are also individually unique and irreplaceably precious. Doesn't that make life for each of us a marvellous gift of creative opportunity to add beauty and goodness to the universe?

For readers who live by faith in a divine creator, the magnificence is no less stunning. To look at ourselves in that light is to look at something that is not only part of the amazing process of cosmic evolution spoken of by science from the Big Bang to this very instant. It is also to look upon life as something that arose in the heart and mind of a God of perfect goodness, who has provided us all with a universe where there is both order and scope for change, hardship as well as comfort, and therein an opportunity to find out for ourselves who we truly are and where we will most truly be at home. To embrace life in this way is to understand the great spiritual cry of St Augustine, that powerful North African Christian of long ago, when he wrote that God has made us for himself and that our hearts are restless until they rest in him.

Whether by reflecting on the story told by science or the one told by the prophets and sages of the world's 'soulscapes', the process of building our moral power begins best, I believe, when we come to see and affirm ourselves as unique centres of creative energy, with the potential to bring the warmth and light of generosity, truth and beauty to life, or to burden and disfigure it with selfishness and untruth.

Step 2: Committing ourselves to enhanced character building

Affirming ourselves as persons with the potential for a life of generosity and integrity, rather than greed and dishonesty is, in itself, only the threshold of ethical living. Essential though it is, the important thing is to *cross* this threshold into a world of practical and effective ethical living. This is what step 2 is about: the decision we all face as to what kind of person we want to see in the mirror: worthy or unworthy, generous or greedy, morally fit or selfishly flabby, two-legged reptile or caring human?

Here it helps to deepen our understanding of the power of choice. One of the ethics workshops that I give deals with this very issue. I begin by taking the group through a typical day and then a typical life, listing what happens and checking it against two factors, which I call biology and choice. The former happens whenever we do something because our bodies are programmed to do it (such as breathing). Choice begins whenever we make a decision that leads to activities of various kinds. Here is my version of this exercise for a typical day for people more or less like me:

Event	Explanation
Wake up	Biology – we can't choose to sleep more than so many hours
Wake up at 06h00	Choice – by setting my alarm clock
Get up promptly	Choice
Drink water	Biology
Shower	Choice
Eat	Biology
Eat bacon and eggs	Choice
Go to work	Both biology (we all need money to live) and choice – e.g. career
Work hard	Choice
Long coffee-break	Choice
Be nice to people	Choice
Eat	Biology
Phone my friend	Choice
Watch the clock	Choice
Stop exactly at 17h00	Choice
Have a drink	Choice

Have family time	Choice
Eat	Biology
Watch TV	Choice
Sleep	Biology

The point is clear: some basic things in life happen whether we want them to or not, but many others are matters of choice, and they have a *crucial influence on the character of our lives.* This makes it vital to understand that we can steer our lives in chosen directions. We must of course sleep, drink and eat, but we can choose whether to do so in excess or moderately, whether to eat healthy foods or junk, and so on.

This power of choice is especially important in relation to others. Because life is through and through relational, there is no way we can avoid having contact with others. But it is up to us whether we will do so helpfully and pleasantly, or in harmful and nasty ways.

Thus we all stand at a fork in the road: will we be part of the world's joy, or part of its pain? Will we walk through life on the path of wisdom and true, lasting well-being, giving more than we take, or will we walk the way of greed and selfish gratification, more concerned about pleasure now for ourselves than anything else? For thoughtful people who have come to understand how human existence works, there is only one answer: embrace the generous option and commit yourself to building your own character in order to foster the enjoyable, durable flourishing that we all want to experience.

Step 3: Being clear about basic values
Living in the power of conscience, as we saw in the previous chapters, is based on a real, sustained commitment to the values that our shared human nature and humanity's long moral experience on this planet have shown to be right and good. Most of us live by these values (at least for some of the time) without thinking much about them because of the way we were shaped when we were young. To add real value to our lives, to start building our personal moral capital, requires more

than this habitual ethic. It requires that we know the main moral values that have stood the test of time in most and maybe even all cultures and societies.

As was explained in Chapter One, I propose the following basic moral principle as the foundation of a life of care, concern and integrity: Ethical living means active concern for the lasting well-being of whoever and whatever we affect, as well as concern for ourselves individually and the future selves we could all be, as the right and good way to live.

The key word 'well-being' stands, of course, for a comprehensively fulfilling life, and not only individual physical gratifications. As we saw in Chapter Four, this principle summarises a set of core moral values, which need to be practised if there is to be genuine, humane growth and a happier world. For convenience, I repeat them here:

Beneficence values	*Integrity values*
Generosity	Truthfulness, which involves:
Respect	Reliability
Fairness	Trustworthiness
Inclusiveness	Self-knowledge
Moral effort	Open-mindedness
Freedom	Judicious criticality
Beauty	Wisdom

In daily life, character building means basing what we decide, what we then do, and how we do it, on these values and not their opposites. How this is done depends very much on what we encounter, which brings us to the next step that we need to take in order to give effect to the commitment to fostering ethically rich contacts in whatever contexts we find ourselves.

Step 4: Mapping our own moral space

The fourth step is intended to make us more aware of the contexts in which we live, especially those where we have a direct influence. Who and what do we affect most directly? Who or what has greatest impact on our lives at this time? This step identifies the main players and other factors in our daily lives. We can think of it as the mapping of our personal moral space. Typically the main players will be a husband, wife or partner, children, parents, maybe domestic workers, immediate colleagues at work (both junior and senior to us), our pets, the natural and built environments we live and move in, and so on. The players will be different for every individual, so it is mostly up to each person to do the necessary moral mapping, but here is an example for readers who might want one:

- the context we share with a life-partner;
- the family group;
- the workplace and city;
- our natural environments;
- our national contexts;
- our cultures, with their belief- and value-systems;
- and ultimately, the global context we share with the whole earth.

There is no way to include every conceivable member of our personal moral space in this list. The main thing is to include everyone and everything on which we have a *direct* influence, and that has a direct influence on us – in other words, things that we can change for the better, to a greater or lesser extent. But at the same time, let us not lose sight of the fact that we are also affected – sometimes very strongly – by quite distant players. The policies of the US government in the Middle East and in stem cell research are a case in point. And who is to say that a well-worded letter to the president won't make a difference? If each individual agrees to do what he or she can, the effect can be enormous – seen clearly in global movements for change, such as the anti-apartheid movement. Individual action can have a powerful ripple effect, as Edmund Burke once pointed out: 'All that is required for evil to flourish is that good men do nothing'. We touch here on the vital issue of moral leadership, which is absolutely essential if we are to enhance moral fitness, even in individuals. This is why I devote a separate step – step 9 – in this programme of personal transformation to moral leadership and management. All the same, charity begins at home, according to the old saying, so a programme of ethical enrichment even for presidents, prime ministers and chief executive officers must begin with personal moral enhancement, not because they or any of us are bad (though some are) but because we can all be better people.

Step 5: Identifying the values that apply most in our personal space
Once we have mapped out the sets of relationships and influences in the various contexts of our lives, the way is open to ask what values are most appropriate or necessary for them to flourish. Here especially, the creative effort of each person is needed, for we alone know the details of our contacts and contexts, and we are thus best able to see what they need from us.

What I can suggest is a device that I find useful in this context. I take a sheet of paper and draw up a matrix or table with a list of key contacts and contexts written down the left side of the page, with the ones closest to me, such as my family and colleagues at work entered first because of their importance to me, and with the set of central moral values entered across the top of the page. Then I work down the list of my relationships, reflect on them and check the values I find necessary for each one. This is not to be confused with a self-check, which comes in the next step. Rather, its purpose is to set out my range of relationships in connection with the set of core values, pinpointing the qualities of character most relevant to each relationship.

For example, my innermost circle involves my wife and our home environment, followed by a circle involving our grown-up sons and daughter-in-law, the gardener who helps us each week, and our dog. Then there is the circle of my applied ethics colleagues at work. Less frequent contacts with friends, neighbours and relatives give me a third circle, while the other staff at the university where I work, being members of my professional organisation, come next. City, province, nation, region, and ultimately the whole planet are the ever-widening circles of concern that make up my personal moral space, with key individuals and organisations in them that affect me, and which I can also affect.

Step 6: Running an ethics audit on ourselves

Now comes the time when we must be especially honest with ourselves. How are we doing? How do we rate in terms of ethical quality on each of the core values? Let's take generosity as an example. In practice, it takes many forms: compassion in response to suffering, loyalty to friends, faithfulness towards one's husband, wife or partner, deep care and proper provision for one's children, kindness and thoughtfulness towards colleagues at work, and so on.

Readers are strongly encouraged to track the many forms of generosity for themselves, and so too with the other values, in relation to each of their contexts of life. It is worth remembering to include the global context of worldwide challenges and ethical problems, asking where we stand in regard to them and how our patterns of life are helping or harming them. For example, are we careless or even profligate in our use of fossil fuels and water, both of which face looming shortages? Are we as generous, kind and helpful to others as we could be? Do we ever make any real sacrifices for others? Are we as honest as we could be?

Having asked these questions, we need to rate ourselves in relation to those closest to and most dependent on us first, and then to the rest of our most significant others, and not only to other human beings. We can do this in any way that proves personally helpful – from an intuitive recognition that we as managers, for instance, can show more concern for our staff, or as parents spend more time with our children, and less time playing golf or bridge – to more systematic ratings on a five-point scale, from excellent to awful, if that is what will help us best.

An analogy from personal financial management may help at this point. There is no need for most of us to take full stock of our financial situations every day, but we do need a thorough review at regular intervals – every month or quarter, for instance. An ethics self-check is a similar exercise. From time to time, it is necessary to look long and hard at our performance, though never in the mode of a stern or unforgiving task-master. This merely undermines the kind of ethic that I am proposing, which aims at growth, fulfilment and zest for life. This kind of frank self-check opens the way to an effective moral action plan, just as it does with personal financial management where, every now and again, changes will probably be needed.

This brings us to the whole point of the ethics audit – identifying what seems sound and what needs to be improved, making a note of the areas within our power to change where the need is greatest. While this involves steps we can and should take to ensure greater truthfulness, fairness or responsibility, it is also helpful to identify ethical problems where we are on the receiving end, such as a lack of respect or encouragement, or sexual harassment at work, and to mark them down for action too.

Step 7: Drawing up and implementing an action plan

The ethics audit gives us a prioritised basis for immediate but carefully considered action to enhance the quality and worthiness of our lives. Even the best of us need to do this because there is always room for added moral value, as with excellence in other aspects of our lives, such as physical fitness or weight control. After all, what kind of person is going to be satisfied with mediocrity in connection with conscience?

Why is it important that the actions we take should be carefully considered? It is possible to be well meaning but end up making things worse if we don't think sensitively about whatever we resolve to improve. I remember, for example, a situation some years ago at the height of the charismatic movement then sweeping across parts of the church. A young priest, very much caught up in this movement, who was trying to do better, bluntly told his unsuspecting superior that he had disliked him all along, but now wanted to change that, guided by the Holy Spirit!

The superior was naturally deeply hurt and very guarded thereafter in his dealings with the young priest.

The point is this: we have to be ethical about ethics itself, which means that whatever steps we take in a sincere desire to add value to our actions must harmonise with the core values to which we are committed, and not contradict or undermine them. Both our *intentions* and the *process* must meet these norms. As in the example given above, insensitively blurting out a hurtful truth because there isn't enough careful consideration can do more harm than good. Here too, we see how truth and generosity need each other.

As for acting promptly, as always, there is no time like the present. The Russian writer Alexander Solzhenitsyn concluded his 1970 Nobel Prize Lecture by quoting a Russian proverb that says, 'One word of truth is of more weight than all the rest of the world' (Solzhenitsyn 1973: 55). I see this piece of traditional wisdom as a way of emphasising the personally and socially enriching power that is immediately released by actions based on conscience, whether speaking a necessary truth, or performing an act of kindness. Besides, who of us, in whom concern for others is real, would want to hold back from spending more quality time with our children, when that is what they need from us, or hold back from whatever else we can do right now to add value to our space?

What should we who commit ourselves to an ethic of generosity do about the ungenerous, the mean and the selfish? Remember, the goal is a more caring world, and a more caring world cannot be achieved if good people let bad behaviour go unchecked. So, such behaviour must be firmly and promptly resisted and the perpetrators given an opportunity for a change of heart and action. If this doesn't work, then generosity must take the form of justice, even severe justice, where necessary, in the form of police action, prosecution and punishment for the guilty. I do not believe that the death penalty and mutilation could be included in the measures that justice can ethically include, lest such actions degrade and dehumanise.

Step 8: Monitoring and persevering

There is no need to get neurotic about a programme of personal moral growth by taking our moral pulses every hour. But, like physical fitness, this area of human growth does need to be checked periodically. Most of us lead busy lives and the best intentions and plans, like New Year's resolutions, can easily be overtaken by the demands of the workplace and the home. So it is wise to build into our programme a resolve to take time out every few months (or whatever interval suits our needs) and assess our situation afresh, using the sort of audit described above.

Above all, we must understand that although we can all make a real difference right now to something, overall growth in the quality of life takes time and perseverance, as with physical fitness; it is a process. This allows our values to embed themselves ever more deeply into our lives so that they truly become part of our characters.

Like many other people, sometimes, when I think of the violence, greed, corruption and crime that fill our news media, I wonder if our moral efforts really can turn the tide against such large-scale evils. At such times, it is important to remember that the defeat of slavery, or progress against racism and sexism, also seemed impossibly daunting, but this did not deter people from taking even small, first steps to overcome them. It is also helpful to remember that conscience becomes its own reward, and that there is something selfish and unrealistic about only being willing to do the right thing if we get quick, visible results.

So I like to pause from time to time under the shade of a large tree, such as a Cape chestnut or an oak tree, and think gratefully of the unselfish, unknown benefactor who planted it, without any expectation of ever enjoying its shade and mature beauty. Experiences like this have helped even an impatient soul like me to plant such trees myself.

Step 9: Making our controlling powers humane and truthful

Sooner or later, in one way or another, everybody manages something or somebody – our marriage partnerships, family life, work situations for which we are responsible, and even entire organisations. For a small number of people, the leadership of entire nations, global corporations and large religious bodies brings with it the power to help or harm vast numbers of people, sometimes for whole lifetimes and even longer.

There are times for everyone when a leadership role must be played. For all of us, therefore, there are powers of control that need to be handled in ways that foster generosity, integrity and genuine well-being in those under our authority. Enhanced ethical living means committing ourselves to a caring and truthful management of those under our authority in any way, from the most minimal and short-lived to the most influential.

I have emphasised in this chapter that conscience grows when character and context are both addressed and can strengthen each other. This means that a great deal of responsibility rests on the shoulders of all who exercise leadership, and particularly on the shoulders of the president of the USA, whose powers affect the entire planet more potently than those of any other single leader. The challenge to leaders such as this is to make absolutely every effort to bring about societies and ultimately a planet so structured at every level of life that inclusiveness, understanding, generosity and truthfulness all thrive and their opposites are curbed, prevented, transformed and where necessary, as a last resort, appropriately censured and punished.

This reality – of the critical importance of ethically supportive contexts – is, perhaps, the most important lesson of the famous Milgrim experiment in California, which showed that even decent people will cause serious pain to others when placed in a context where powerful figures and social arrangements so require (Milgrim 1974). This, however, is not news to those of us who have lived under evil regimes. We know how an unjust and cruel national context can turn otherwise decent and God-fearing people into willing agents of those regimes. We understand why Hitler could thrive – albeit only for twelve years – in a country that had produced leaders, thinkers and artists of the calibre of Luther, Kant, Goethe and Bach. So we know that when an entire society is controlled in unjust and even brutal ways, which always entails the use of fear because of the ever-present threat of violence against dissidents, as well as the control of information, then otherwise good and sincere people mostly conform to the iron rule of their context. They may even come to believe that what they are serving is good and noble. This is why in South Africa, we saw people rising from their knees and emerging from their churches, and then inflicting apartheid on their fellow South Africans.

This is also why truly ethical democrats (as distinct from those who use the language of morality but miss its depth and substance) in the USA and the world over are so deeply disturbed by what can be seen from the White House under the leadership of President George W. Bush: an administration that seems to have forgotten the superb wisdom of a generation ago that I, along with hundreds of others, heard from a brave and inspiring Bobby Kennedy, when he visited South Africa in 1966 – that you cannot defeat evil by imitating its methods, but only by means of a superior goodness – a goodness that involves respect, fairness, generosity and friendship, not domination.

Whatever the level and the kind of control that we exercise, the goal is always the same: to lead, manage, and influence, not only effectively, but also well. The entire message of this book is that to do anything well, we must do it with generosity of spirit and action, and with integrity. In short, to handle our powers of control and leadership well, we must handle them on the basis of a rich, all-embracing conscience. So the basic question that we who exercise some kind of control have to ask ourselves is whether we are using that power mainly for our own personal gain, or for the benefit of all whom we affect – as judged and approved by them, and not only by us.

As always with conscience, we must be very honest with ourselves in answering this question, but also gracious – meaning that when we summon the courage to admit to ourselves just how selfish we really are in dominating our marriages, families, businesses or nations, we do so as an essential step towards committing ourselves to greater active concern for those under our authority. We therefore also need an audit of the ways that we use whatever powers of control we may have, just as we do for the rest of our actions, asking ourselves, and wherever possible, those whom we influence, exactly what benefit they get from the way we use our powers, and also what harm they may be suffering. We need to know what is sound about our leadership and then continue or improve it, and what is harmful and thus in need of change – including the harm we may be doing to ourselves, remembering always that while despots are despised and eventually dumped, true democrats are respected and followed.

Step 10: Sharing and enjoying the results
One of the most attractive features of conscience, of moral goodness, is the way it makes a visible, tangible and enjoyable difference to the well-being of those we influence, as well as our own. Replacing a hurried, overly busy presence that never stops to take a real interest in those around us with a friendly, helpful presence at work and at home makes a difference that we can all feel and relish. For example, it eases and relaxes things for others, and that makes the spaces we move through each day more enjoyable for us too. Thus the moral quality of our lives as shown by our concern for others and our integrity enriches whatever contexts we influence.

Demonstrating real integrity, appreciation and fairness in the workplace allows others to trust us and be loyal to us. This in turn means a greater likelihood that they will give of their best, just as we saw in Chapter Three in connection with the two great options we face as to how to relate to others – the way of selfishness and greed, or the way of generosity and concern for the well-being of others. Most of us will find the experience of actively wanting others to find fulfilment very pleasant. Thus moral wealth increases the more we spend it, which is another reason why it makes such excellent sense to invest heavily in such wealth. Even better, nobody can ever rob us of it, though we ourselves might squander it.

The overall result of more and more of us living lives based on a rich, strong conscience, lives marked by the values explained in this book, is a world less wounded than it is now, a world of much greater and richer well-being for more and more people – maybe, in the end, for us all. What could be more worth devoting our lives to than such a vision?

Nor should we become despondent in the face of all the news we get daily about unethical behaviour, some of it gross in the extreme, such as a baby being raped, or the bomb-shattered children in Baghdad. Acts of individual moral goodness – kindness, brave honesty, loyalty when others back away, or a determination not to let go of moral resolve because others may cheat – these seemingly little achievements, are seen and felt by others whom we may never know. They win from such people a welcoming response and real encouragement to do likewise. So they gather momentum and ripple onwards to others. That is why one word of truth, or one act of kindness, outweighs the whole world.

Lest this seem no more than a utopian dream, here is the proof. Gandhi was a completely unknown and untried young lawyer on the night in May 1893 when he was thrown off a whites-only railway carriage at Pietermaritzburg station in South Africa because of the colour of his skin. His response to this experience was a commitment to find a better way that could overcome racism and violence. This response began as no more than a thought in the mind of the unknown young lawyer he was then. From there, it led to actions that at first affected no more than a handful of friends. This 'experiment with truth', as Gandhi later called it, won commitment from his friends. This produced the beginnings of a new kind of moral movement, which in time would help India to become independent, the USA to achieve civil rights for its black citizens, and South Africa to overcome apartheid without horrific bloodshed.

As Margaret Meade, the well-known anthropologist reportedly once said, according to a postcard I found in an Oxford shop run by an international aid agency, 'Never doubt that a small group of thoughtful, committed citizens can change the world. Indeed, it's the only thing that ever does'. And all it takes is the first practical step to add value to the space where we can all make a difference.

So, I would like to end by inviting readers to embrace this superb opportunity to turn the tide of greed, cruelty and corruption that has been showing its ugly face so disturbingly of late around the world. Let us be freedom fighters for a generous, just and truthful world, taking it back from the forces of greed and violence we can all hear invading the streets, workplaces and homes of our lovely but wounded world. Together, we can make all the difference in the world.

Epilogue

I end this book by bringing together, as concisely as I can, the values that I believe will give rise to greater global flourishing, the same values that history's great streams of conscience have carried to the four corners of the earth:

- Be actively concerned for the well-being of all whom you affect.
- Resist the pull of selfish desire.
- Care especially for the weak, the poor, the vulnerable, and the innocent.
- Live honestly, respectfully, justly, and with integrity.
- Seek always to understand.
- Enfold sexuality with love, faithfulness, responsibility, and respect.
- Use freedom kindly.
- Protect the earth and all living things.
- Add beauty to the world.
- Live as friends.

Select Bibliography

Ashbrook, James B. and Carol Rausch Albright. 1997. *The Humanizing Brain: Where Religion and Neuroscience Meet*. Cleveland: The Pilgrim Press.

Baker, John Austin. 1971. *The Foolishness of God*. London: Darton, Longman and Todd.

Blackburn, Simon. 2001. *Being Good: A Short Introduction to Ethics*. Oxford: Oxford University Press.

British Medical Association. 1998. *Human Genetics: Choice and Responsibility*. Oxford: Oxford University Press.

Brown, Judith M. and Martin Prozesky. 1996. *Gandhi and South Africa: Principles and Politics*. Pietermaritzburg: University of Natal Press.

Buber, Martin. 1958. *I and Thou*. Edinburgh: T. & T. Clarke.

Burkill, T.A. 1971. *The Evolution of Christian Thought*. Ithaca: Cornel University Press.

Bush, George W. 'President's Remarks at the National Day of Prayer and Remembrance'. The National Cathedral, Washington, DC, 14 September 2001. http://www.whitehouse.gov/news/releases/2001/09.print/20010914-2.html (accessed 10 October 2006).

Carson, Clayborne (ed.). 1999. *The Autobiography of Martin Luther King, Jr*. New York: Little, Brown and Company.

Chadha, Yogesh. 1998. *Rediscovering Gandhi*. London: Arrow Books.

Craig, Robert. 1963. *Social Concern in the Thought of William Temple*. London: Gollancz.

Crook, John H. 1980. *The Evolution of Human Consciousness*. Oxford: Clarendon Press.

Cupitt, Don. 1995. *Solar Ethics*. London: SCM Press.

Dawkins, Richard. 1989. *The Selfish Gene*. Oxford: Oxford University Press.

De Gruchy, John W. and Martin Prozesky. 1991. A *Southern African Guide to World Religions*. Cape Town: David Philip.

De Waal, Frans. 'The empathetic ape'. *New Scientist*, 8 October 2005: 52ff.

Dosick, Wayne. 1998. *Golden Rules: The Ten Ethical Values Parents Need to Teach Their Children*. San Francisco: Harper Paperbacks.

Elion, Barbara and Mercia Strieman. 2001. *Clued up on Culture: A Practical Guide for South Africa*. Cape Town: One Life Media.

Esack, Faried. 1997. *Qur'an, Liberation and Pluralism: An Islamic Perspective of Interreligious Solidarity Against Oppression*. Oxford: Oneworld.

Fernandez-Armesto, Felipe. 2004. *So You Think You're Human?* Oxford: Oxford University Press.

Fletcher, Joseph. 1966. *Situation Ethics: The New Morality*. London: SCM Press.

Frankena, William K. 1973. *Ethics*. Englewood Cliffs, N.J.: Prentice-Hall, Inc.

Free Inquiry 23(4), October/November 2003.

Gandhi, M.K. 1990. *An Autobiography or The Story of my Experiments with Truth*. Ahmedabad: Nevajivan.

Geering, Lloyd. 1980. *Faith's New Age: A Perspective on Contemporary Religious Change*. London: Collins.

——. 1991. *Creating the New Ethic*. Wellington: St Andrew's Trust.

Gensler, Harry J. 1998. *Ethics: A Contemporary Introduction*. London and New York: Routledge.

Giddens, Anthony. 1998. *The Third Way: The Renewal of Social Democracy*. Cambridge: Polity Press.

Gilligan, Carol. 1993. *In a Different Voice: Psychological Theory and Women's Development*. Cambridge, Massachusetts: Harvard University Press.

Glover, Jonathan. 1999. *Humanity: A Moral History of the Twentieth Century*. London: Jonathan Cape.

Gobodo-Madikizela, Pumla. 2003. *A Human Being Died that Night: A South African Story of Forgiveness*. Boston: Houghton Mifflin Company.

Griffin, James. 1986/1988. *Well-Being: Its Meaning, Measurement and Moral Importance*. Oxford: Clarendon Press.

Hamer, Dean. 1994. *The Science of Desire: The Search for the Gay Gene and the Biology of Behavior*. New York: Simon and Schuster.

——. 2004. *The God Gene: How Faith is Hardwired into our Genes*. New York: Doubleday.

Hammond-Tooke, W.D. (ed.). 1974. *The Bantu-speaking Peoples of Southern Africa*. London: Routledge & Kegan Paul.

Hanson, N.R. 1969. *Perception and Discovery: An Introduction to Scientific Inquiry.* San Francisco: Freeman, Cooper & Co.

Harvey, David. 2003. *The New Imperialism.* Oxford: Oxford University Press.

Haseler, Stephen. 2000. *The Super Rich: The Unjust New World of Global Capitalism.* Basingstoke: Macmillan.

Hick, John. 1989. *An Interpretation of Religion: Human Responses to the Transcendent.* London: Macmillan.

Hinde, Robert A. 2002. *Why Good is Good: The Sources of Morality.* London and New York: Routledge.

His Divine Grace, A.C. Bhaktivedanta Swami Prabhupada. 1972. *Bhagavadgita: As It Is.* New York: Collier Books and London: Collier Macmillan Publishing.

His Holiness the Dalai Lama. 1999. *Ancient Wisdom, Modern World: Ethics for a New Millennium.* London: Little, Brown and Company.

Holm, Jean and John Bowker. 1998. *Making Moral Decisions.* London and New York: Pinter Publishers.

'Humanist Manifesto 2000' in *Free Inquiry* 19(4), Fall 1999: 4–20.

Hurtshouse, Rosalind (ed.). 1995. *Virtues and Reasons.* Oxford: Oxford University Press.

Jenkins, David E. 1969. *Living with Questions: Investigations into the Theory and Practice of Belief in God.* London: SCM Press.

Joas, Hans. 2000. *The Genesis of Values.* Cambridge: Polity Press.

Kant, Immanuel. 1933. *Critique of Pure Reason.* Translated by Norman Kemp Smith. London: Macmillan.

Kidder, Rushworth M. 1994. *Shared Values for a Troubled World: Conversations with Men and Women of Conscience.* San Francisco: Jossey-Bass Publishers.

——. 2005. *Moral Courage.* New York: William Morrow.

King, Ursula M. (ed.). 1995. *Religion and Gender.* Oxford: Blackwell.

——. 1998. *Faith and Praxis in a Postmodern Age.* London: Cassell.

Kitson, Alan and Robert Campbell. 1996. *The Ethical Organization: Ethical Theory and Corporate Behaviour.* London: Macmillan.

Küng, Hans. 1997. *A Global Ethic for Global Politics and Economics.* London: SCM Press.

Küng, Hans and Karl-Josef Kuschel (eds.). 1993. *A Global Ethic: The Declaration of the Parliament of the World's Religions.* London: SCM Press.

Küng, Hans and Jürgen Moltmann. 1990. *The Ethics of World Religions and Human Rights.* London: SCM Press.

Küng, Hans and Helmut Schmidt (eds.). 1998. *A Global Ethic and Global Responsibilities: Two Declarations.* London: SCM Press.

Kurtz, Paul. 1988. *The Ethics of Humanism*. Buffalo: Prometheus Books.

Lazlo, Erwin. 1972. *The Systems View of the World*. New York: George Braziller.

Levy, Neil. 2004. *What Makes us Good? Crossing the Boundaries of Biology*. Oxford: Oneworld.

Milgrim, S. 1974. *Obedience to Authority*. London: Tavistock.

Morgan, Peggy and Clive Lawton. 1996. *Ethical Issues in Six Religious Traditions*. Edinburgh: Edinburgh University Press.

Morrison, Reg. 1999. *The Spirit in the Gene: Humanity's Proud Illusion and the Laws of Nature*. Ithaca: Cornel University Press.

Murove, M.F. 1999. 'The Shona Concept of *Ukama* and the Process Philosophical Concept of Relatedness, with Special Reference to the Ethical Implications of Contemporary Neo-Liberal Economic Practices'. Unpublished MA dissertation, University of Natal, Pietermaritzburg.

Murphy, Nancy and George F.R. Ellis. 1996. *On the Moral Nature of the Universe: Theology, Cosmology and Ethics*. Minneapolis: Fortress Press.

Murray, David. 1997. *Ethics in Organizations*. London: Kogan Page Limited.

New Oxford Dictionary of English. 1998. Oxford: Oxford University Press.

Nussbaum, Martha. 2000. *Women and Human Development*. Oxford: Oxford University Press.

Penelhum, Terence. 2000. *Christian Ethics and Human Nature*. London: SCM Press.

Phillips, Helen. 'The cell that makes us human'. *New Scientist*, 19 June 2004: 32ff.

Pinker, Steven. 2002. *The Blank Slate: The Modern Denial of Human Nature*. London: Allen Lane.

Prozesky, Martin. 1984. *Religion and Ultimate Well-Being: An Explanatory Theory*. London: Macmillan and New York: St Martin's Press.

——. 1995. 'The philosophical anthropology of Alfred North Whitehead'. *South African Journal of Philosophy*, 14(2): 54ff.

——. 1999. 'Ethics in Process Perspective'. *South African Journal of Philosophy*. 18(1): 1ff.

Richards, Janet Radcliffe. 2000. *Human Nature after Darwin: A Philosophical Introduction*. London: Routledge.

Ridley, Matt. 1997. *The Origins of Virtue*. London: Penguin.

Rolston, Holmes, III. 1999. *Genes, Genesis and God: Values and their Origins in Natural and Human History*. Cambridge: Cambridge University Press.

Ruether, Rosemary Radford. 1996. *Women Healing Earth: Third World Women on Ecology, Feminism and Religion*. London: SCM Press.

Ruland, Vernon. 2002. *Conscience Across Borders: An Ethics of Global Rights and Religious Pluralism*. San Francisco: University of San Francisco Press.

Russell, Bertrand. 2004. *Power: A New Social Analysis*. London: Routledge.

Sacks, Jonathan. 2002. *The Dignity of Difference: How to Avoid the Clash of Civilizations*. London: Continuum.

Sagan, Carl and Ann Druyan. 1992. *Shadows of Forgotten Ancestors: A Search for Who We Are*. London: Century.

Schweiker, William (ed.). 2005. *The Blackwell Companion to Religious Ethics*. Oxford: Blackwell Publishing.

Scott, Ted and Phil Harker. 1998. *Humanity at Work*. Luscombe, Queensland: Phil Harker & Associates.

———. 2002. *The Myth of Nine to Five: Work, Workplaces and Workplace Relationships*. Sydney: Richmond.

Shutte, Augustine. 2001. *Ubuntu: An Ethic for a New South Africa*. Pietermaritzburg: Cluster Publications.

Singer, Peter. 1981. *The Expanding Circle: Ethics and Sociobiology*. Oxford: Clarendon Press.

———. 1983. *Hegel*. Oxford: Oxford University Press.

———. 1993. *Practical Ethics*. Cambridge: Cambridge University Press.

———. 1993/1997. *How Ought we to Live? Ethics in an Age of Self-Interest*. Oxford and New York: Oxford University Press.

———. 1999. *A Darwinian Left: Politics, Evolution and Cooperation*. London: Weidenfeld and Nicolson.

Smart, Ninian. 1973. *The Religious Experience of Mankind*. London: Collins/Fontana.

Solzhenitsyn, Alexander. 1973. *Nobel Prize Lecture*. London: Stenvalley Press.

South African Concise Oxford Dictionary. 2002. Cape Town: Oxford University Press.

Sutherland, Stewart. 1996. *Education, Values and Religion*. The Victor Cook Memorial Lectures. Centre for Philosophy and Public Affairs, University of St Andrews.

Theissen, Gerd and Annette Merz. 1998. *The Historical Jesus: A Comprehensive Guide*. London: SCM Press.

Thorpe, S.A. 1991. *African Traditional Religions*. Pretoria: University of South Africa.

Tobias, Phillip V. 1981. *Evolution of Human Brain, Intellect and Spirit*. Adelaide: University of Adelaide.

Warnock, Mary. 1998. *An Intelligent Person's Guide to Ethics*. London: Duckbacks.

Whitehead, A.N. 1929/1978. *Process and Reality: An Essay in Cosmology*. New York: The Free Press.

———. 1933/1967. *Adventures of Ideas*. New York: The Free Press.

———. 1938/1966. *Modes of Thought*. New York: The Free Press.

Williams, Bernard. 1993. *Morality*. Cambridge: Cambridge University Press.

Wilson, E.O. 1975. *Sociobiology: The New Synthesis*. Cambridge, Massachusetts and London: The Belknap Press.

———. 1998. *Consilience: The Unity of Knowledge*. London: Little, Brown and Company.

Wright, Robert. 1994/1996. *The Moral Animal: Evolutionary Psychology and Everyday Life*. London: Abacus.

Yankelovich, David and William Barrett. 1971. *Ego and Instinct: The Psychoanalytic View of Human Nature – Revised*. New York: Vintage Books.

Zohar, Danah. 1991. *The Quantum Self*. London: Flamingo.

Index